Ken Russell's

Ken Russell was a successful ph̲.̲.̲.̲g̲.̲.̲p̲.̲.̲.̲ ̲b̲e̲.̲ ̲e̲ ̲being hired as an independent filmmaker by the BBC. Between 1959 and 1970 he made thirty-five 35mm films for the BBC that advanced the art of filmmaking in England and which are still mostly unavailable. He enjoyed worldwide box-office success with *Women in Love* (1969), *The Music Lovers* (1970) and *Tommy* (1975) and, in Britain in the 1970s, he had more number-one hit films than any filmmaker. Ken Russell made the last great (and least expensive) M.G.M musical, *The Boy Friend* (1971). His 1971 feature film, *The Devils* is increasingly recognised as being the boldest and the finest film made by an Englishman.

Paul Sutton is an historian and photographer in Cambridge. His books include *Lindsay Anderson, The Diaries* (Methuen & Bloomsbury); *Becoming Ken Russell*; *Talking about Ken Russell*; *Understanding Gary Numan,* and the two-part novel *Charlie Ellis and the Day Trip to Mars.*

Ken Russell by Paul Sutton

Ken Russell's
Dracula

With an Introduction
by Paul Sutton

Buffalo Books
Cambridge UK

Ken Russell's Dracula
© Ken Russell Productions, 2009

Introduction
© Paul Sutton, 2012
camerajournal@hotmail.com

The moral rights of the author of the screenplay,
and of the Introduction have been asserted

3rd Edition February 2017

Published by Buffalo Books
Cambridge, UK

ISBN: 978-0-9572462-1-8

Contents

Introduction

"I've heard you have written a screenplay for *Dracula*. There isn't a film I'd like to see more than *Ken Russell's Dracula*. Can you tell me something about it?" were the very first words I ever said to Ken Russell. It was shortly after 4pm on Sunday 11th June 1989. He was on the stage at the City Lights cinema in Nottingham. I was in the audience. The cinema, built at the top of a small Sixties high-rise, was closing down. The owners had decided to go out with a bang and had programmed a dozen days of 35mm prints of Ken Russell films, from *Elgar* and *Song of Summer* on Tuesday 30th May, through to *Dante's Inferno, French Dressing, Women in Love, The Devils, Savage Messiah, Altered States, Crimes of Passion, Salome's Last Dance, Gothic* and *The Lair of the White Worm*, to conclude on Sunday 11th June with Ken Russell himself live on stage. Thereafter the cinema would be knocked down. On stage with Russell was Christopher Gable, the star of *Song of Summer, Dance of the Seven Veils* and *The Boy Friend*. When I asked my question, Gable and Russell looked at each other almost conspiratorially. Russell said to Gable. "Should I tell him?"

"Go on," said Gable.

"Okay. I've come up with a version of *Dracula* that makes sense of the story. If you had lived for centuries, would you go weak at the knees at a picture of a dull clerk's fiancée and lock yourself away in a gloomy castle? I wouldn't. I've come up with a reason why Dracula would want to live forever."

Russell explained his theory, then added: "The film won't get made. It was killed off by Larry and Langella [Laurence Olivier and Frank Langella]. When I was touting my script round the studios there were three other *Dracula* scripts in development. 20th Century Fox picked the dullest (the Larry and Langella) because they thought it was safe. It had been a hit play on Broadway. They picked a bland American actor to be their Dracula. Mick Fleetwood (Fleetwood Mac's drummer) was going to be mine."

Twentieth Century Fox distributed Werner Herzog's *Nosferatu* (1979). The Langella *Dracula* was produced by Universal. That same year UIP released *Love at First Bite* (1979), a Dracula comedy starring

George Hamilton, that proved to be the most profitable of the three. The catalyst for the Ken Russell version was four men: John Hawn, who had invested money in a screenplay development company; James V. Hart, who had persuaded Hawk to option a coffee table book called *The Annotated Dracula* by Leonard Wolf; Bobby Littman, Russell's American agent, who had earned his spurs, when he was MGM's top man in Europe, by buying *Savage Messiah* for the company and hiring Russell to make *The Boy Friend*. The fourth man was Michael Nolin, an acquisition consultant at Columbia pictures.

Nolin remembers: "I wanted to make a film with Ken Russell. Bobby Littman needed to get a job for Ken Russell. We made a deal and Ken went to work on the screenplay. I gave Ken a copy of *The Annotated Dracula* which he thought was great. Mick Fleetwood was never ever seriously considered by Ken for the role. Ken had to be coerced into even meeting him. After *Valentino* and *Lisztomania*, the last thing Ken wanted was a film starring a non-actor. The cast we envisioned went something like this: Peter O'Toole as Dracula (I don't know if O'Toole was ever formally approached, but at the time he was almost as unemployable as Ken. Littman knew his agent well); Michael York or possibly Alan Bates (a Littman client) as Harker; Mia Farrow and Sarah Miles (both Littman clients) as Lucy and Mina. Oliver Reed (a Littman client and an actor "prepared to eat bugs" for Ken) as Renfield. James Coburn (a Littman client) as the American cowboy. Peter Ustinov (a friend of Littman's) as Van Helsing. We couldn't make offers to any of these actors at this stage because we didn't have any money, but that is the type of cast Ken wanted and that Littman and I spoke about to foreign sales companies. Against Littman's advice, John Hawn bought a two-page ad in *The Hollywood Reporter* and (I think) *Variety* announcing *Ken Russell's Dracula*. Universal had started thinking about a movie based on their play. I don't know if the ad hastened the development of their project, but it certainly didn't help."

The young Hawn was a Fleetwood Mac fan. "John Hawn was obsessed with Fleetwood Mac," says Nolin. "When it dawned on Hawn that Ken had made *Tommy*, he saw *Dracula* as a chance to meet the band. He got word out to Mick Fleetwood that Ken was considering him as an actor. When Ken found out he was appalled and enormously pissed-off. Hawn had gone so far as to get Ken invited to a Fleetwood Mac concert in Landover, Maryland, where Mick Fleetwood would meet him backstage. Ken refused to go, and only relented because Littman wouldn't let Hawn be embarrassed this way. We all flew to Landover but the concert was cancelled two-and-a-half hours after it was supposed to begin (Lindsay Buckingham had a drug overdose or an epileptic fit of some kind). Ken was in a foul mood, having flown in from England for a concert he didn't want to see. Russell met Fleetwood either that night or the following morning. We had a plane to catch and Fleetwood, being a rocker, was late for the meeting. When Ken asked Mick if he had done any acting, Fleetwood acknowledged that he hadn't even had a lesson, but he said he'd think about drinking actual blood to prepare for the part. Ken nearly bust a gut."

That same day, Ken Russell met the producer, Martin Poll in New York City. "Poll had a foreign sales company and, not coincidentally, had his greatest success with *The Lion in Winter* starring Peter O'Toole," says Nolin. "We got confirmation that Universal were rushing their play-based *Dracula* into production starring Frank Langella. Martin Poll's interest in Ken's film went away because there would be no profit in being the second *Dracula* in the marketplace. Years later, James V. Hart, who was passionate about making the first 'real' *Dracula* film actually based on the novel, sold his own spec. screenplay to Francis Coppola."

Ken Russell moved on to make *Altered States* (1980), a film about transformation, and the search for the origins of self; a film about man's connection to eternity.

The first time I went to Ken Russell's home, then a thatched 16th century house within a 17th century rose garden, on ancient hunting grounds deep within the forest on the South Coast of England, we talked through his whole career, from his early days as a stills photographer (he photographed Richard Burton on location in Spain for *Alexander the Great* in 1956) to the mid-price digital film, *Elgar Revisited* (2001), that he was preparing to make for the *South Bank Show*. The conversation had reached *Song of Summer* (1968), Russell's perfect film about a young man who travels to a foreign land to work for a strange and violent old man who feeds on the young man's lifeblood, creatively sucking him dry. Ken Russell frowned when I mentioned the name of the actor who played the young man - Christopher Gable. Gable had died in October 1998 at the horribly young age of fifty-eight. It wasn't Gable's death that had stirred Russell's emotion. Their friendship had broken down before Gable died. Gable had hurt Russell. They had not been reconciled. "What did he do to hurt you, Ken?"

"He stole my ideas for *Dracula*. He used them in a ballet. He didn't ask my permission and he didn't acknowledge my contribution."

Was my innocent question on that wonderful day in Nottingham the catalyst for the breakdown of their friendship? Did I plant the seed in Gable's mind to 'steal' Russell's ideas? I kept quiet and moved the discussion to an easier topic, the wholly unique *Dance of the Seven Veils* (1970), Russell's feature-length dance film about Richard Strauss that has the horrible distinction of being the second Ken Russell film to be banned worldwide after a single screening. The BBC had disgraced itself by bowing down to the humourless, artless heirs of Richard Strauss. It is still banned.

On returning to Cambridge, I set about researching Gable's *Dracula*. He had produced it for the Northern Ballet Theatre, where he was the artistic director, and he had staged it at Sadler's Wells, the London theatre where he had first found fame as a dancer. (From the Royal Ballet at Sadler's Wells, he moved to the Royal Ballet at Covent Garden where, in 1965, he made the national papers by being usurped from the world première of Macmillian's *Romeo and Juliet* by a dark and famous exile from the East, Rudolph Nureyev). I found an original advertising poster for Gable's *Dracula* at Sadler's Wells. On the poster was clearly written 'based on an idea by Ken Russell'. Press articles released at the time also mentioned Ken Russell's name. I telephoned Russell and said: "Ken, I've found a poster for Chris's *Dracula* at Sadler's Wells. Your name is on the poster. He did acknowledge you. He didn't try to pass off your ideas as his own. I can send you the poster if you want me to?" Ken didn't want the poster, but he did seem less angry with Gable.

I did not see Gable's production of *Dracula* on its original release, and I have not seen any of the continuing revivals, but extracts from the revivals are on youtube, and there are descriptions of the production in the press of the day. I must admit I can't see any resemblance to Ken Russell's version. There hasn't been anything like Ken Russell's version.

I wrote to Philip Feeney, the ballet's composer. He replied: "I was aware of the estrangement between Christopher Gable and Ken Russell, and had an inkling that it was about *Dracula*. And it's certainly true that Christopher was something of a magpie, taking inspiration from many eclectic and multicultural sources, and I am sure he would have been very excited by Ken's ideas. For my part, I had no knowledge of the Russell script, and was surprised at the detail of its nature which you give, especially as you point out, Northern Ballet Theatre latterly made a point of saying that it was inspired by an idea by Ken Russell, when its content seems so different. As far as I could see, the NBT production of the mid-1990s was strongly based on the Bram Stoker novel, and pretty much follows it through until the chase at the end of the novel, which Gable and Pink thought wouldn't work as a ballet, and substituted a substantial Blood Mass scene, giving the vampires a nice dance opportunity, which van Helsing *et alia* gatecrash, and get their man. I actually don't remember Ken being referred to very much, if at all, in those legendary concept meetings at Christopher's house. These tended to be dominated by Lez and Christopher, indeed, in my experience, design and plot generally take centre stage in these meetings (I guess because it harder to instantaneously envisage either choreography or music before they actually exist)."

In 1992, I was living in deep and darkest Gloucestershire. The nearest shop was seven miles away. I was thinking it was about time I learned how to drive. Francis Ford Coppola's *Dracula* came to the new multiplex in town so I got on my bicycle and pedalled ten country miles to see it. I had a great time. It's a wholly enjoyable silk and shadows silent-movie trick film with acknowledged nods to Abel Gance and F. W. Murnau (whose *Nosferatu* (1922) was almost lost to us when all known copies were destroyed following a lawsuit brought by a sorry bunch of work-shy heirs with 'claims' to Stoker's estate). Coppola's film is amusingly flawed by the audacity of casting two young Americans as Harker and Lucy and allowing them to attempt English accents. One of the film's many strengths is Coppola's Count played by Gary Oldman as a Japanese version of Rachel Roberts in *Picnic at Hanging Rock* (1975), Peter Weir's quietly interesting film about schoolgirls disappearing in the wilds of Australia. Oldman would follow *Dracula* by starring as Beethoven in *Immortal Beloved* (1994), a film by Bernard Rose that had the distinction of having been 'stolen' from an unmade script by Ken Russell. 'Hi, Ken, sorry I stole your script', wrote Rose in an article published in *The Guardian* newspaper on 15th September 2008. Now I'm about to give away a major surprise from *Ken Russell's Dracula*, so if you are reading this before reading the script, and you don't want to know what happens in the script, then skip the rest of this introduction.

In Russell's *Dracula*, Dracula thrives through immortality by being a great artist who, over the centuries, keeps his secret by changing his persona and by mastering all the arts from love to music and painting. He is Casanova. He is Beethoven. He is Sibelius. He is Picasso. Which should keep Gary Oldman gainfully occupied.

After having had such a good time watching Coppola's *Dracula* I treated myself to a VHS festival of Francis Ford Coppola films, respectfully not including his masterpiece *Apocalypse Now* (1979) which, with its 6-track magnetic soundtrack and its Technovision visuals is not a film to watch on VHS (Coppola told *Rolling Stone Magazine* that *Apocalypse Now* would be "like a Ken Russell film"). I tried and failed again to see why some film critics think *Godfather 2* (1974) is a better film than the peerless original. I enjoyed the High School blood and tumble of *The Outsiders* (1983, the grand orchestral version scored by Carmine Coppola); Mickey Rourke in the refreshingly expressionist *Rumblefish*; and I re-watched Kathleen Turner miscast in *Peggy Sue Got Married* (1986, a film I had previously seen on a ship going to Denmark). Turner is much better in her previous film, Ken Russell's *Crimes of Passion* (1984), 'better' being defined as 'in every possible way'. Curiously, Russell made *Crimes of Passion* at Coppola's Zoetrope studio, and enjoyed a vacation at Coppola's Californian vineyard. I didn't like Turner's Stepford Wife performance in the Coppola film but it won an Oscar nomination, as did the cinematography by Jordan Cronenweth. Cronenweth had been doing TV and no-budget films in Hollywood until Ken Russell almost hired him for *Valentino* in 1976, when Hollywood was gearing up for its first Ken Russell film. After interviewing and rejecting Coppola's discovery, Al Pacino, for the role of Valentino, and seeing and rejecting all the crews in Hollywood, Russell announced that, with the exception of Cronenweth, he hadn't seen anyone who could hold a candle to his crew back in England so he made the film in England. English unions stopped Russell from hiring Cronenweth and forced him to use a cinematographer with a British union card, Peter Suschitzsky, who subsequently became David Cronenberg's right hand man.

When Russell finally did agree to make a film in Hollywood, the grand metamorphosis spectacle that is *Altered States*, the cast and crew had already been hired by Arthur Penn. Penn, the original director, had walked from *Altered States* because he couldn't work with the constant interference from and temper tantrums by the film's writer, Paddy Chayevsky. Russell, who had first met Chayevsky in London in 1959 (as told in my book *Becoming Ken Russell*), solved the Chayevsky problem by promising not to change a single word of the script if, and only if, Chayevsky went back to New York City. With Chayevsky out of the way, Russell allowed all of Penn's cast and crew to stay with three major exceptions. He replaced the special effects chief, *Star Wars* maestro, John Dykstra, because Dykstra wanted to do the special effects in miniature when Russell knew and would show that they would be better done 'for real'; he brought in his own editor, Stuart Baird (who has since made an invaluable career in Hollywood applying his Russell-learned skills to rescue many-a blockbuster, including *Star Wars, Rogue One*), and Russell insisted on hiring Jordan Cronenweth. With *Altered States*, Russell and Cronenweth initiated the 'look' that Cronenweth would take to his second major film, *Blade Runner* (1982), the most gloriously photographed science-fiction film of all.

None of the Coppola films which followed *Dracula* seemed worth a twenty-mile bicycle ride over Cotswold hills, even for a young man country-starved of culture, so I didn't see another Coppola project until 2001, not long after my first visit to Ken Russell's house. Academia had come a-calling and I was living in Cambridge. At the end of my postgraduate studies I had founded and was editing *Camera Journal*, the Cambridge University Film Journal. The first issue was a Lindsay Anderson special edition. The second was a Ken Russell special (I had wanted the first to be about Ken Russell but Russell said: "Let's see an issue first"). That was the reason for my visit to his house. I was interviewing him for the journal. He was doing his accounts. His table was spread with legal documents.

At that time, a horror film called *Jeepers Creepers* was attracting a lot of attention partly because it was said to be very good, partly because Francis Ford Coppola was its producer, but mostly because the press disapproved of the man Coppola had hired to make it. Coppola had put his name and reputation on the line by hiring Victor Salva. Salva had committed a crime against a young actor on a previous film, had served jail time for that crime, and had shown remorse. Coppola had hired Salva because he thought Salva was the best man for the job. Coppola's Catholic-Christian upbringing had taught him that forgiveness and redemption are essential parts of civilised life. The American press, and it seemed from the way it was being reported, much of the American public, disagreed. The American press and public believed that if a man committed a crime then he should be tarred with that crime for the rest of his life. Coppola stood by his Christian values and, in interview after interview, he stood by the man he had hired.

This made the news in England, a country which then still prided itself on having *Christian values.*

Out of curiosity, and respect for Coppola's stance, I went to see *Jeepers Creepers.* I was amazed. It was the most enjoyable horror film I'd seen since the heyday of the genre-redefining films of Dario Argento and Lucio Fulci. Coppola had indeed hired the best man for the job. *Jeepers Creepers* is about a teenage brother and sister driving through the countryside and being terrorised by a man-bat which collects human body parts, and which lives in a deconsecrated chapel dressed with the preserved nude corpses of his mostly young male victims. 'Jeepers Creepers where did you get those eyes,' sings the film's musical refrain in teasing prelude to the film's cruel coda.

Years later I finally got to read Ken Russell's *Dracula* script, which every Hollywood producer worth his salt had read. 'Jeepers Creepers, Francis, where did you get those ideas?', I thought when I read a scene set in a deconsecrated chapel, to where the nude body of a boy is brought. The scene ends with:

'Dracula is drawn into the whirling
incandescent dust until, with a mighty
beating of oily black wings, he flies
forth through the shattered, gaping
windows into the darkening night,
like a creature from Dante's Inferno.
All faces watch his triumphant flight
in complete awe.'

Which sort of serves as the 'written on the back of an envelope' précis for *Jeepers Creepers 2* (2003).

And Coppola's *Dracula*? Was it an open steal from Ken Russell? After-all, the writer James V. Hart is a link to both? No, Coppola is an artist with his own agenda. He's too good a filmmaker to need to steal a fellow artist's work. Coppola's *Dracula* is Coppola's own, but Coppola was wise enough to learn from the filmmaker whom Don Boyd calls The Master. Boyd produced *Aria* (1987), a portmanteau musical film with sequences directed by Robert Altman, Jean Luc-Godard, Derek Jarman, Ken Russell and others. Russell's sequence, made in much less time than any of the others (he was brought in at the last minute when Fellini dropped out) is the towering highlight of the film.

So what did Coppola take/learn from Ken Russell?

The scene-to-scene changes. We hadn't really seen their like before in Coppola's films (though there's a hint of them in the famous helicopter/air-conditioning-fan aural transition in the opening scene of *Apocalypse Now*). In Coppola's *Dracula*, the camera closes in on the eye of a peacock feather and dissolves to the 'eye' of a tunnel from which a train is emerging; bites on Lucy's neck dissolve to the eyes of a wolf. Attributed to Roman Coppola in Francis Ford's DVD commentary, this device, these transitions, seem to me to be a steal in form but not in content from the Russell's *Dracula* script.

In the thirty-five 35mm films he made for the BBC between 1959 to 1970 (most of which are still suppressed), Ken Russell perfected and advanced the art of the scene-to-scene transition, and of the symbol-to-symbol transitional cut. It reaches an on-screen peak in *Women in Love*, when Russell cuts from a lovemaking couple to a dead couple (the dead man is Christopher Gable) with all four bodies shaped in a matching pose. That transition cut made audiences gasp at the film's première. It still makes audiences gasp. Russell's *Dracula* script contains perhaps the greatest scene-to-scene transition of all. A shot of a steamship on the sea dissolves to a shot of the famous steamship engraved on an *England's Glory* matchbox. The matchbox opens and out crawl insects. An insect is picked out and put into the mouth of the man holding the matchbox: Renfield.

In addition to being a jaw-droppingly great moment of cinema, this transition has added depth and resonance because it references a key symbol within Russell's oeuvre. The *England's Glory* matchbox was used in a pop painting by the artist Derek Boshier and featured in Ken Russell's landmark art film *Pop Goes the Easel* (1962). The matchbox emblem in Boshier's painting is merged on the left by the stars and stripes of America. The painting is a symbol of the transference of American ideas into English culture. Russell owned Boshier's most famous painting, *Man Playing Snooker and Thinking of Other Things* (1961, which also features in *Pop Goes The Easel*). Depending on what mood Russell was in when he told this story, the painting was taken by or given to his wife, Shirley, in 1978, the year they divorced, the year he wrote *Dracula*. Through Sotheby's, Shirley Russell sold the painting to The Berado Museum in Lisbon. The Boshier reference in the script thus becomes a symbol too of the transference of Ken Russell's property; a sort of Harker-Dracula arrangement. (Boshier told me he only leant the painting to Russell and was shocked it was sold. He'd leant it partly because Russell's London house had walls big enough to exhibit it).

Was Coppola's use of Ken Russell's symbolist scene transitions a nod that the roles have reversed, that America is taking Irish-English culture (Stoker, Russell) to inform new American art? And are Coppola's transitions drawn from incidents in Coppola's own life? I doubt it. Which is a reason why Coppola's work, for all its decorative riches, operates at a lower and lesser level than vintage Ken Russell.

In 1987, having burned all his bridges in Hollywood by refusing to tug his forelock to frankly incompetent studio executives, and for refusing to make *Evita* because 20th Century Fox were insisting he used a stage actress, Elaine Paige, whom three Oscar-winning cameramen (including Billy Williams and David Watkin) couldn't make look right on film, Ken Russell offered the *Dracula* script to Vestron, a fledgling production company who had risen out of video distribution and who had offered him a three picture deal. Russell knew that 'video' was the future of 'film'. (In 2001, he would become the first major filmmaker to self-finance a digital feature film). Vestron had attracted Russell's attention by profitably distributing *Gothic* (1986) in the States. They liked the *Dracula* script but they couldn't afford to make it. The maximum budget they could raise and offer him was less than $2 million. So, for less than $2 million, Ken Russell made them a horror-comedy based not on Bram Stoker's best book but on his worst, *Lair of the White Worm* (1988). If you want the best, you have to pay for the best.

On 13th February 1989, four months before answering my question in Nottingham, Ken Russell met Mick Fleetwood at the Royal Albert Hall in London. Fleetwood was co-presenting the Brit Awards, a televised shout-and-scream ceremony for pop teens. At the show, Fleetwood wore Dracula black. Russell arrived on stage in a white satin jacket to tear open a golden envelope and to announce that the winner of the award for the Best Video was Michael Jackson. Of course, Russell had no idea that his next appearance in a lowbrow 'teen popular' entertainment show, a full eighteen years later, would involve sharing a *Big Brother* house with Michael Jackson's brother, Jermaine.

On the subject of coincidence, the first Ken Russell film to be banned worldwide after a single screening was his Chaplinesque comedy *Diary of a Nobody* (1964), the first of his films to feature his famous company of players, including Murray Melvin, Brian Murphy (*The Devils, The Boy Friend*), Bryan Pringle (*French Dressing*) and the great Vivian Pickles (*Isadora Duncan*). The wee and gross heirs of Weedon & George Grossmith complained that Russell's film made the low-middle-class comic prose of their ancestor's book seem low-middle-class and comic. The BBC, who commissioned the film, disgraced itself by bowing to the Gross demands and withdrawing the film for the rest of Ken Russell's life (with the exception of five screenings over four decades at the National Film Theatre in London). The BBC, who still refuse to allow the film to be screened on television, or sold to DVD or download, have since spliced footage cut from the film into several cut-and-paste tele shows such as *Faulks on Fiction*.

So why bring that up in an introduction about Dracula? Bram Stoker was a part-time writer but a full-time man of the theatre. He was a full-time friend of Henry Irving. It can be said with certainty that aspects of Irving's character inspired the more cultivated aspects of Dracula's character, and an Irving-as-Dracula reading does tie nicely with Ken Russell's version. Stoker was with Henry Irving when Stoker made the 'eureka' visit to Whitby, the English seaside town with the ruined abbey on the rocks that gave him the inspiration for Dracula's castle. Irving and Stoker were in Whitby to meet a writer whose play had flopped in nearby Scarborough. The writer? George Grossmith.

Let's look at Ken Russell's script:

Russell's prose style has a lot of energy and an almost total disregard for the conventions of punctuation. Clauses and sentences run into each other wilfully, as if Russell is suggesting a moving camera. Certainly his narrative style creates a flow of images. In publishing the script, I've left the punctuation alone with the exception of adding forty or fifty commas where they are needed to clarify meaning. These are mostly where Russell had neglected to put a comma before a name. For example, he writes: "That's enough Professor", which suggests the speaker has had his fill of Professor for tea. A comma before the word Professor makes it clear that the speaker is telling the Professor to stop doing what it is he is doing.

It's curious to observe the decline in the standard of dialogue given to Harker, in the first instance, and then to Van Helsing. Harker starts out speaking the complex sentences of an educated man, but soon declines into a sort of Cockney. On reaching Vienna, in the pursuit of Dracula, Van Helsing's English deteriorates into a schoolboy imitation of a foreigner, with simple sentences ending with the verb, e.g. 'He would an embarrassing spectator be'. I've left this in, if only because it gives a rare screen example of pre-*The Empire Strikes Back* Yoda-speak.

The only really new characters Russell adds to the Dracula story are a nurse called 'Danvers', doubtlessly after Hitchcock's lesbian housekeeper in *Rebecca* (1940), and the aforementioned boy, The Gardener's Boy. Dracula uses the nude boy to entice Renfield. Unlike his lapsed Catholic contemporary, Pier Paolo Pasolini, whose work seemed to be awash with naked youths, and which Russell found abhorrent (he told me that Pasolini's *Canterbury Tales* was the most disgusting film he'd seen), the young male nude was not something with which Russell liked to dress his sets.

An earlier use of a boy in a nude scene had got him into a lot of trouble. During the filming of *The Devils*, the parents of a 14-year-old extra sold a story to the dirty Sunday newspapers that their son was filmed romping about with two naked nuns. This kiss-and-tell story caused such an uproar of excitement in Fleet Street that *The Devils* was swept up into a destructive tidal wave of cant and outrage from which it can't properly recover, for much of the 'excitable' footage was then destroyed. The name of the *Devils* boy is Balfour Sharp. Balfour is such an uncommon name that it's quite likely that the only other Balfour Russell had heard of was Balfour Gardiner, a minor British composer. Ken Russell was a national authority on minor British composers. A punning flourish on Gardiner's name, whilst winking at the rats of Fleet Street who seemed to praise Pasolini's films to the skies, and the boy in *Dracula* was born. Renfield is Fleet Street.

It should be remembered that a script isn't a film. It's the building block, the bare bones if you will, for a film. On the whole, Ken Russell did not slavishly adhere to the written script, the major exception being *Altered States*, and even there, the highlights, the hallucinations, were Russell's invention and were not in the script. The nuns stripping off in the pit, and Balfour's romp in *The Devils* (if indeed it took place), were improvised on the day. *Ken Russell's Dracula* would be polished through with added colour. Ideas would flow and changes would be made after casting and during the design process and the filming. That said, the script is a finished piece of Ken Russell work. If he was a composer it would be given a full Opus number. It exists. It is real. A reading of it will probably give more film-pleasure than any trip to the local multiplex.

But if I were producing a film from the script, and I was back at Russell's house before it burned down, mysteriously, in 2006, I'd ask him to rewrite it to clear up a lack of consistency in the characterisations of Dracula and Harker, and the knock-on effect this has on the looseness of the themes. Harker starts off as a dynamic young man issuing commands, full of righteous indignation at the treatment of the poor. On meeting Dracula, Russell comes up with the idea that Harker should be a Little-Englander clerk. The idea of presenting Count Dracula as a great European man of arts and culture fighting against little philistine Englishmen is a good one, but Russell doesn't develop it much beyond a reference to England as 'A godless kingdom of the plebian' (when Dracula's hires a New Forest chapel that was sacked by Cromwell) and there's a hint in the finale when a Public School-type uses cricket skills in a comedy attempt to dispatch the Count's gypsies (the English education system has long been divided between *admired* sportsmen and *despised* aesthetes).

Russell's Dracula is set in the 1920s, the decade in which he was born, and the decade he loved best. It's the decade of great silent cinema (Gance, Murnau, Chaplin, Lang) and the decade of the settings for *Women in Love, The Boy Friend* and *Valentino*, the last of which is told in flashback from a coffin, the story of a film icon who has metamorphosed across the arts and into Rudolph Nureyev.

Stoker's in-England scenes are changed from Whitby to Russell's home county of Hampshire, specifically the city of Southampton where he was born, and from where the Titanic sailed (Dracula's steamship arrives crashing into the iceberg that's Southampton pier), and to the neighbouring New Forest where Ken Russell lived, loved and died. Quincey is remodelled into a Douglas Fairbanks action-hero, a characterisation which adds the silent cinema sub-theme common to many of Russell's films, and works well alongside the exotic Dutch Europeanism of Van Helsing. Lucy is no longer just a pretty face. She's an opera star dying from leukaemia, a big improvement on Stoker's characterisation and which gives Dracula a reason to fall in love with her. The film has spectacle and a lot of humour. It has the best opening and closing scenes of any adaptation, and too few moments of horror. The moments of horror-themed spectacle are drawn mostly from Stoker, but these are mostly coloured 'tongue-in-cheek' by one element that Russell brings to the table - a lot of imaginative silliness. Russell's adaptation of Stoker's *The Lair of the White Worm* (1988) strikes the same tones.

Ken Russell's Dracula is, in fact, the absolute opposite of Werner Herzog's *Nosferatu* (1979) which partially scared off the funding for Russell's film. Herzog's is a horror film on the theme of loneliness.

Herzog's Dracula wants to die. Ken Russell's Dracula wants to live forever, a great and gregarious artist. That's the idea, but it isn't very evident in the script. The implication from the script is that Dracula is responsible for creating the Aubrey Beardsley-style bedroom where Harker spends his first night, but imitation is not a hallmark of greatness (the suggestion isn't there that Beardsley was Dracula). We see Dracula *listening* to music by Schubert. We see him *watching* from the wings at what we can presume will be a gloriously imagined staging of Tchaikovksy's fiery opera, *The Maid of Orleans* but it is not made clear that Dracula was the man who created them. In Russell's script, he's a consumer not a creator.

But Russell would say, 'What about the Pop Art statue of the blood fountain of youth which Harker stumbles on during his escape?'.

And I'd say, 'I don't like it, Ken, and it's not enough. We need to see Dracula at work on his arts and crafts.'

I'd be admiring the full wall collage of pop art images of Saints and the Madonna which Russell had made for his entrance hall. I'd have eaten a welcoming meal of roast chicken and I'd be drinking a glass of fine Tokay, and I'd say, 'It's asking too much of the audience to imagine that Dracula made it. We need to know that he's a great artist. His tragedy is that he has to destroy Life to create Art.'

I'd ask: 'Is he going through a visual art phase or is he a musician? Is he a filmmaker?'.

'A filmmaker?'

'You've set it in the Twenties, Ken. Could Dracula be Murnau? Fritz Lang? Chaplin? We could see him turning the handle of the camera as his stage-managed horror starts to unfold?'.

Then I'd pause, because the truth would dawn on me that Russell is at least one step ahead. Ken Russell's Dracula is a cloaked portrait of Ken Russell himself. And I'm sitting in his house, looking through a few legal documents for him. The day has darkened. And I'm a long way from home.

Ken Russell's
Dracula

EXT. A STREET IN BISTRITZ. NIGHT.

A young man encumbered by a heavy suitcase in one
hand and a bulky briefcase in the other fights his
way along a sidewalk crowded with people dressed in
the national costume of Transylvania which reflects
the meeting of two cultures - East and West. The
flustered traveller, hot and perspiring in a new
overcoat is JONATHAN HARKER, a handsome if somewhat
gauche young Englishman lost in a new world of
strange sights and peculiar customs, such as the
procession confronting him at the moment.
Giant articulated bats operated by masked mummers
flap and flutter down the main street flanking the giant
figure of a sinister medieval prince belching coloured
smoke from his ears and exploding firecrackers from
his mouth as the town band plays a mournful dirge.
Jonathan takes the carnival in with only fleeting
glances and is obviously looking for a landmark,
which he soon finds in the shape of an old clock
tower, at the foot of which waits a liveried COACHMAN
seated on a beautiful open caleche and holding the
reins of three fine white horses.
Jonathan approaches the Coachman who jumps down and
bows respectfully.

COACHMAN   Herr Harker is it, ya?

JONATHAN   Good evening, yes. You are to take me
              to Count Dracula, yes?

COACHMAN   Whenever you wish, Herr Harker.

JONATHAN (briskly) There's no time like the present.

He goes to enter the carriage but although the
coachman has hold of the door handle he hesitates
to open it.

COACHMAN   I'm sure his Excellency the
              Count would not object if you
              broke your journey here and
              continued on tomorrow, much
              refreshed, Herr Harker.

23

                        I understand you have come all
                        the way from England and the
                        Golden Crown has a first-class
                        cuisine and the finest gypsy
                        band in Bistritz.

JONATHAN (eagerly) Business before pleasure!
                        It's most thoughtful of you but
                        I'd rather press on, thank you ...

But still the coachman seems reluctant to open the
door.

JONATHAN   ... er, the sooner the better.

The coachman's formality slips away as he takes
Jonathan into his confidence and talks to him man to
man.

COACHMAN   Please sir, do you know what day it is?

Jonathan is puzzled yet growing impatient with the
delay.

JONATHAN   The Fourth of May, 1925.
                And unless we get a move on,
                it will soon be the Fifth.

COACHMAN   It is the Eve of St. George's Day.
                Tonight when the clock strikes
                midnight all the evil things
                in the world will have full sway.

Jonathan finally realizes that it is the Coachman's
fear rather than concern for his comfort which is
the real issue.

JONATHAN (condescendingly) My dear good fellow,
                        where I come from, ladies sell paper
                        roses in the street on
                        St. George's Day and donate
                        the proceeds to a charity for
                        homeless children. There's
                        nothing to be frightened of
                        I assure you. After all, he
                        is our patron saint you know.

The Coachman bows his head and, admitting defeat, opens the door at last and assists Jonathan into the carriage.

COACHMAN   Herr Harker is fortunate to live
in such a civilized country.
Our homeless children have their
own begging to do.

He nods at a couple of scruffy URCHINS who are pestering Jonathan with trinkets, then gives them a rough shout and a cuff on the head. This annoys Jonathan who has taken a positive dislike to the Coachman.

JONATHAN   Hey, steady on ...
(calling out to the
retreating children)
Here ...

He offers them a couple of coins, as the Coachman, with a look of disapproval, hauls Jonathan's luggage on board. The Urchins thank Jonathan and stuff a trinket in his hand.

JONATHAN   No, I don't want ...

Too late - they have disappeared into the darkness before he has a chance to return ... a rosary. To throw away such an object, which is obviously alien to his beliefs, would seem ungracious so he stuffs it in his pocket and settles down to his journey. As the Coachman guides the carriage through the crowds Jonathan sees, with some satisfaction, a carnival float representing St. George slaying the dragon.

JONATHAN   There! What did I tell you?
Our chap will soon put paid
to your bogies.

But his laughter is not shared by the Coachman who crosses himself and steers the horses away from the friendly light of the carnival towards the darkness of the country beyond.

EXT. COUNTRY ROAD. NIGHT.

Moonlight shining through slender pines lulls Jonathan
into a romantic mood as the carriage jogs gently
towards majestic snow-capped mountains until flames
flickering through the trees break the reverie.

JONATHAN   Driver, do you see that -
             not a forest fire is it?

In reply, the Coachman urges his horses into a fast trot.

JONATHAN   No, I see people... what's
             the hurry, aren't gypsies
             friendly around here?

COACHMAN   No, gypsies ... not friendly. Evil!

By now the coach is drawing level with the flames
and the strange ritual they illuminate. Jonathan's
curiosity turns to alarm.

JONATHAN'S POINT OF VIEW:

Cloaked and hooded FIGURES with flaming torches surround
an altar on which some fiendish ceremony is being
celebrated involving a naked WOMAN. A PRIEST holds
a silver chalice in readiness while another brandishes
a knife aloft as if invoking a blessing from the
darkness. A blood-curdling scream cuts through the
night as the knife plunges into the heart of the
sacrificial victim. Blood pours into the chalice
which is raised in thanks and then drunk by the
officiating priests. Now the trees thicken up and,
with a last brief flicker of light, the scene disappears
from view.

RESUME: INT. CARRIAGE.

Jonathan, stricken with horror by what he has just
witnessed, rises swaying to his feet and grabs at
the Coachman in desperation.

JONATHAN   My God! Did you see that?
             Is there nothing we can do?

The Coachman refuses to be involved and doesn't even turn his head.

COACHMAN   Nothing!

JONATHAN   Go back to Bistritz -
(angrily)   we must inform the police.
                  I order you.

Slowly, the Coachman turns around with a growl. He has changed into a WEREWOLF. Jonathan's blood chills in his veins as the Werewolf snarls, showing his gleaming fangs. Jonathan acts quickly and snatching up the whip from its holder, jumps to the back of the carriage and lashes the beast across the shoulders causing it to roar in pain. Once again Jonathan lashes out but this time the beast is too quick and tearing the whip from Jonathan's grip hurls it into the road and jumps at him with flashing claws. Jonathan ducks and the claws merely rip his coat, but the next moment man and beast are locked in a deathly struggle... and just when it seems the Wolfman must tear out his throat, Jonathan gets his knee into its chest and heaves with all his might, toppling the beast over the edge of the carriage and into the road where he rolls over in the dust howling with rage.
Jonathan's next thought is to get the horses under control. Accordingly he starts clambering into the swaying driver's seat as the vehicle continues its headlong career. It is then he sees yet another astounding sight. A PEASANT GIRL has collapsed on a rock at the edge of the road and pants in delirium as a vampire bat, wings quivering, sucks blood from her jugular vein. Before he has grasped the reins she is a vanishing figure in a nightmare where his own survival is the keynote. As he strives unsuccessfully to check the runaway horse, he becomes aware that his flight is taking him through a wood of dead fir trees on the spiky trunks of which are impaled a number of LUCKLESS MEN, WOMEN and CHILDREN whose screams mix with the howling like the hounds of hell.
Over his shoulder he sees that a pack of wolves are in hot pursuit. As the leaders snap at the flying hooves, the horses thunder across a drawbridge and into the courtyard of:

CASTLE DRACULA.

Round the yard they gallop with the howling pack in
hot pursuit until, suddenly, someone is standing
in their path. It is the figure of a MAN IN BLACK
who must surely be trampled down by the crazed
steeds. But the burning eyes and hypnotic will of
the man prevail over the fear of the plunging horses
who halt inches before him, trembling, snorting and
foaming with exhaustion. But there is still another
danger to contend with.

JONATHAN   Save yourself ... the wolves!

And indeed the wolves are almost upon the man in
black who bears an uncanny resemblance to the carnival figure of the Medieval Prince seen in Bistritz.

MAN IN BLACK/DRACULA Down Berserker. Good boy. Down!

To Jonathan's astonishment, the wolves behave like
lambs and frisk around their master who feeds them
lumps of sugar and treats the exhausted Jonathan to
a warm, disarming smile.

DRACULA   I am Dracula, welcome to my home.
             Enter freely and depart in peace,
             leaving something of the happiness
             you bring.

He treats Jonathan to a good-natured laugh in which
he is joined by a number of PEOPLE in smart evening-
wear pouring from the big open doors which lead to
a brightly-lit hallway. Jonathan doesn't know if he
is awake or dreaming, it is impossible to reconcile
recent horror with present laughter.

JONATHAN   I've just seen ... fearful
             things... your driver ...

DRACULA   A versatile fellow, Lazlo -
             coachman, chauffeur, actor ...

With a wave of his arm, he turns to the archway
through which purrs a Rolls Royce Silver Wraith. As

it draws to a halt, Jonathan recognizes with disbelief the Werewolf at the wheel and, by his side, the Peasant Girl waving a rubber vampire bat. They are laughing and chattering, obviously enjoying themselves no end.

DRACULA   And this is Katya, our little
                 sewing maid. Now off with you
                 to the servants' hall - the
                 party's in full swing!

At this, Lazlo takes off his werewolf mask and, waving it in the air, drives off down a ramp into the bowels of the castle. Meanwhile, the Count takes Jonathan by the arm and leads him through the doorway.

INT. CASTLE DRACULA. THE GREAT HALL. NIGHT.

As Jonathan takes in the decor which, to his surprise, contrasts greatly with the medieval exterior of the building, being the last word in 1925 contemporary, Dracula leads him past a throng of COUPLES dancing to a jazz band towards a sweeping marble staircase.

DRACULA   This is a country of feast days
                 my friend and we celebrate them all,
                 rich and poor alike. Down in Bistritz
                 you saw a peasant carnival which has
                 remained unchanged for centuries.
                 Up here we pay tradition a
                 more sophisticated tribute.
                 Most festivals have a -
                 sacrificial victim, Mister Harker.
                 I'm afraid you were the martyr
                 of our little hoax tonight.

He puts his hand on his heart and smiles charmingly but Jonathan is not to be so easily placated.

JONATHAN   Some joke, with my ruddy coat
                 nearly torn off my back.

Dracula notices Jonathan's torn coat and general disarray.

DRACULA   Was that Lazlo?

JONATHAN (nodding tersely) Well, I don't make
a habit of calling on new clients
dressed like a tramp!

DRACULA (sympathetically) He plays too rough.
Next year I will have to give him
another role.
(he examines the torn cape)
You will be reimbursed.
In the meantime, Katya will
attend to it. Now please say
we are forgiven?

JONATHAN (good-naturedly) I'm in your debt, Count.
I'm now England's leading
authority on Transylvanian
folklore.

DRACULA   Let me get you a drink.

JONATHAN   Er, thank you. Anything will do.
What's your poison?

DRACULA (puzzled) My what...? Oh...
(he sees Jonathan looking at his ruby glass)
... your English slang. This
is a local beverage known as
Bull's Blood. An acquired
taste. Not to everyone's
palate I'm afraid. Here...

He whisks a large brandy from the tray of a passing
WAITER and hands it to Jonathan.

DRACULA   I think you'll be happier with this.

JONATHAN   Mmmm ... thank you. This'll
warm the cockles.

Dracula leads Jonathan up a broad staircase to the
first floor, making polite conversation as he goes.

DRACULA   Have you always been in
Real Estate, Mr. Harker?

30

JONATHAN   Ever since I was demobbed,
                yes, Count.

DRACULA (puzzled) De-mobbed ...?

JONATHAN   Er, yes... demobilized.
                I was at the front in the war,
                the Royal Yorkshires.

DRACULA   The War! Such senseless
(frowning)   bloodshed! Here we are ...

They reach the head of the stairs and stop at the
first doorway. Dracula opens it and ushers Jonathan
into:

INT. THE BEARDSLEY ROOM. NIGHT.

DRACULA   I thought you'd be at home here.

JONATHAN (startled) Blimey!

Judging by Jonathan's expression, he has never seen
anything like it. Life-size reproductions of Aubrey
Beardsley's more erotic works adorn the walls. The
furniture also is moulded on the artist's phallic
style, while the drapes and fabrics are in stark
black and white.

DRACULA   Beardsley was surely one of your
                finest artists. It is to my
                ever-lasting regret that I
                never met him. So talented,
                and to die so young. A tragedy!
                I might have helped him.

JONATHAN   Are you a doctor, sir?

DRACULA (laughing) I dabble a little in acupuncture,
                certainly; I'm also something of
                a patron of the arts. Now, I must
                return to my guests, forgive me.
                I hope you will join us later?

JONATHAN   That's very nice of you, Sir,
                but I think I'll turn in if
                it's all the same. I'm proper
                fagged out.

Dracula is quite relieved having marked Jonathan down
as far beneath him both socially and intellectually.

DRACULA   Of course. I think we have
                anticipated your needs, but
                should you require anything
                ... simply ring.
                (He indicates an electric bell)
                Business can wait till after
                lunch when we will hopefully
                exchange contracts. In the
                meantime this will help you
                sleep well and dream well.

He pours some amber coloured liquid from a decanter
into Jonathan's glass.

DRACULA   ... and by the way, you were
                never in the slightest danger.
                You're little use to me dead,
                you know.

Jonathan manages a hollow laugh as he raises his
glass and takes a sip.

JONATHAN   Not to worry, Count. I guessed
                it was a hoax. Pleasant dreams.

The Count smiles to himself and exits leaving Jonathan to knock back his drink, get a refill from the
decanter and take in his surroundings.

JONATHAN'S POINT OF VIEW:

The camera passes over the wallpaper showing four
men with giant erections dancing before an audience
of beautiful women.

JUMP CUT BACK TO REVEAL:

Jonathan in bed gazing at the phallic frieze through blinking, dreamy eyes. No sooner has he turned the light out and settled down to sleep than THREE of the beautiful WOMEN on the wallpaper seem to gradually materialize at his bedside. Through a drugged haze, Jonathan smiles at them. He has witnessed too many bizarre events in one night to question this one.

JONATHAN   On behalf of St. George,
              welcome to my dream, ladies.

Not knowing if he is awake or dreaming and caring less, Jonathan does not resist as the central figure leans languorously forward, eyes glittering seductively as if to kiss him; indeed he longs for it with languid anticipation. Lower and lower dips the girl's head until her lips pass below the range of his mouth and poise above his throat. Jonathan feels the dents of two sharp teeth on his skin with a tremor of ecstacy that is short-lived. Suddenly the door is thrown open revealing the hard silhouette of DRACULA.

Immediately the THREE VAMPIRE GIRLS fall back in terror. Dracula strides towards the bed where Jonathan pretends to be more drugged than is actually the case. Apparently convinced, Dracula turns his attention to the vampires.

DRACULA   How dare you touch him,
              any of you! How dare you vent
              your lust on him when I have
              forbidden it!

The FIRST VAMPIRE WOMAN collects herself and retaliates with a metallic laugh.

FIRST VAMPIRE WOMAN It is you turned our love
              into lust!

SECOND VAMPIRE WOMAN You have never loved!

At this the vampires all laugh, so that the room is filled with a soulless mocking sound frightening in its cruelty.

```
DRACULA          I outgrew your kind of love,
                 long ago. MY love surpasses
                 your understanding. Now GO!

THIRD VAMPIRE WOMAN (hungrily)
                 Are we to have nothing tonight?

FIRST VAMPIRE WOMAN (sarcastically)
                 Would you have us all die?

THIRD VAMPIRE WOMAN (despairingly)
                 Would that we could!

SECOND VAMPIRE WOMAN ... to be freed from this need,
                 this craving for blood.

DRACULA          The blood is the life, the Power,
                 and the Glory. Take it!
```

Dracula points through the door into the brightly lit corridor where a naked BABY is seen crawling on the carpet. Through hazy, half-shut lids, Jonathan just has time to see the three vampire girls leap with a cry at the child before Dracula follows them closing the door behind them. Jonathan hears with a shudder the screams of the dying child gradually smothered by the sounds of greedy sucking until a voice outside the castle ground fetches him swaying from his bed to look out of the window.

JONATHAN'S POINT OF VIEW:

At the foot of the castle wall, quite clear in the moonlight, stands the figure of a beautiful PEASANT WOMAN shouting desperately at someone high above.

```
MOTHER           Monster! Give me my child!
```

BEARDSLEY BEDROOM: Jonathan changes his eye-line.

JONATHAN'S NEW POINT OF VIEW:

Dracula, standing on the battlements, his cloak billowing in the wind, looks at Woman with disdain. Clambering over the battlements, Dracula begins to crawl down the castle wall FACE DOWN with his cloak spreading around him like great wings. He continues until he reaches the hypnotised woman, whose screams turn to cries of ecstasy as Dracula bites through the jugular vein and sucks long and deep.

INT. BEDROOM. NIGHT.

Jonathan turns away from the gruesome sight and, feverishly searching his overcoat, finds the once disparaged crucifix which he hangs around his neck like a talisman. Next he turns to lock the door but, as there is no key, he has to content himself with jamming a chair under the handle before falling onto the bed in a swoon.

FADE OUT NIGHT

FADE IN DAY

INSERT: A cut-throat razor. A hand comes into shot
       and lifts it out of frame.

CUT BACK TO REVEAL:

Jonathan shaving himself with the aid of a small mirror which reflects most of the empty room behind him. Suddenly, a hand falls on his shoulder causing him to jump and nick his chin.

DRACULA   Good day.

Jonathan looks in the mirror again to see how he could have been mistaken. But there is no mistake; everything in the room is reflected - save DRACULA. A trickle of blood runs over Jonathan's chin attracting the attention of Dracula and possessing him with demonic fury. As Dracula makes a grab for his throat, Jonathan pulls away instinctively, knocking over and smashing the mirror while Dracula's hand falls upon the crucifix and rosary beads. Instantly, Dracula checks himself and his fury passes.

DRACULA   Take care, take care how
                 you cut yourself. It is more
                 dangerous than you think in
                 this country.

He turns and heads to the door watched by Jonathan, dumbfounded.

DRACULA   After you have lunched we
                     will conclude out business.

As he exits, TWO SERVANTS enter with a heavily laden luncheon table which Jonathan surveys with little appetite.

INT. CASTLE DRACULA. MUSIC ROOM. DAY.

Large and spacious with portraits of famous musicians adorning the walls, including Beethoven and Sibelius. A phonograph plays a recording of Schubert's 8th Symphony as DRACULA examines photographs of a gracious house and picturesque ruined chapel, while JONATHAN stares at a large portrait of a beautiful woman dressed as Salome and tries to appear at ease in the presence of a man he knows to be a monster. Whether Dracula is aware of this is impossible to say for, superficially, he appears relaxed and affable.

DRACULA   You seem ill at ease, my friend.
                     Is Schubert not to your taste?

JONATHAN (brightly) Ah, Schubert, that's it!
                     I knew I knew that tune.

DRACULA   His Unfinished Symphony.

Jonathan covers up his ignorance and disquiet by attempting a weak joke.

JONATHAN   Pity you weren't around to help him
                     as well. He might have finished it.

To Jonathan's surprise Dracula takes him seriously, warming to him somewhat.

DRACULA   Yes... that is one of the
                     great regrets of my life.

Realizing he has let slip something which should have remained secret, he continues in a lighter vein.

DRACULA   ... but who knows, perhaps I
             would have been too busy saving
             Franz Liszt; misguidedly of
             course.

Dracula abruptly changes the subject and gets down
to business, thus sparing Jonathan the embarrass-
ment of a reply.

DRACULA   You are sure the property
             is secluded?

JONATHAN (reassuringly) Exactly as you requested
             in your letter, sir. It's right in
             the heart of the New Forest, and
             apart from a private sanatorium,
             there's not a soul for miles.
             Your nearest big town is Southampton.

Dracula continues to study the photographs with
enthusiasm as Jonathan fiddles nervously with his
briefcase.

DRACULA   The chapel is a little gem;
             is it consecrated?

JONATHAN (defensively) I'm afraid not, sir -
             sacked by Cromwell's Roundheads.

DRACULA   Cromwell! Ah, fascinating man -
             though something of a tyrant, yes?

JONATHAN   Depends on your politics, sir,
(pompously)   and religion. Personally, I
              think he made England what
              she is today.

DRACULA   A godless kingdom of the
              Plebeian; I concur totally
              Harker. Where do I sign?

Jonathan is somewhat disconcerted not knowing quite
how to take Dracula's last remark.

JONATHAN   Er, quite, sir. Right here please.

37

Dracula signs the document with a flourish.

DRACULA   Thank you, Harker. My bank will
                telegraph the money to your firm
                in Southampton tomorrow.

JONATHAN   On receipt of which, Carfax
                Manor is yours, sir.

DRACULA   Thank you Harker. I took a
                chance. I selected your firm
                from an advertisement in
                your local paper, but it
                seems to have paid off most
                satisfactorily. I am delighted.

JONATHAN   Thank you, sir! It was a
                pleasure doing business with you ...
                (awkwardly)
                Er, if there is nothing more,
                then I'll be packing my things.

DRACULA   You cannot wait to shake the
(chuckling)   dust of Castle Dracula from
                your shoes. You have still not
                forgiven our little joke.

JONATHAN (over-reacting) Not at all, Count.
                It's just ... well ...

Desperately, Jonathan hides his anxiety behind a
half-truth.

JONATHAN   ... well, I can't very well be
                late for my own wedding can I?

As Jonathan forces an awkward smile, Dracula expresses
pure delight.

DRACULA   My dear fellow, you should have
                brought the young lady along.
                What better place for a honeymoon
                than our beautiful Carpathians?

With a sweep of his hand he indicates the mountain peaks
visible through the elegant windows while Jonathan

prepares to demonstrate that he is not the dummy Dracula takes him for.

JONATHAN   She couldn't have got away,
               I'm afraid; she's too busy
               organizing Lucy Weber's
               farewell season.

Dracula follows Jonathan's glances to the portrait of the gorgeous woman, hanging on the wall above them, with a look of total incredulity. For the first time his mask of detached sophistication - slips!

DRACULA   I beg your pardon?

JONATHAN   My fiancée is Lucy's secretary.

DRACULA   You are referring to Lucia Weber
               (pronounced Vayber) the opera star?

JONATHAN   That's just her stage name,
               we've always known her as Lucy.
               Have you met? I've never heard
               her mention you.

Dracula becomes unaccountably flustered. Now it is his turn to be uncomfortable. He chooses his words carefully, not wishing to give away his true feelings.

DRACULA   Er, no. Though I had the great
               good fortune to hear her sing
               once in Budapest. I shall never
               forget it.
               (he becomes genuinely moved)
               And to think that golden voice
               will soon be silenced; it's tragic!

Jonathan, carried away by his own concerns for Lucy, forgets for a moment that he is talking to a man he considers to be a homicidal maniac.

JONATHAN   At least her records will survive.

DRACULA (bitterly) Grotesque caricatures
               to mock her memory.

JONATHAN (philosophically) Everything that can
be done has been done to save her.
She's very brave but it's hopeless.
Her personal physician is preparing
her for the end. All we can do is pray.

DRACULA (cynically) Save your breath, God is deaf.

The hatred in Dracula's voice snaps Jonathan out of
his reverie.

JONATHAN   When I see her, shall I give her
             your regards?

Dracula too is once again on guard. Jonathan Harker
knows far too much. He must be removed.

DRACULA   ... by all means, do!

Jonathan mistakenly feels he is off the hook.

JONATHAN   Well, I'll be saying cheerio then;
             I'll ...

DRACULA (interrupting)
             I'm afraid that will not be possible.

Jonathan's relief drains from his face as Dracula
continues brightly at a rush, almost ad-libbing.

DRACULA   ... you have your patron saint
             to thank for that; it's a public
             holiday. Lazlo will take you to
             Bistritz first thing tomorrow.
             Meanwhile, everything here is at
             your disposal. Why not spend
             the rest of the day in diversion?
             Browse through my library,
             relax in my picture gallery -
             my home is yours; please.

Despite the fact that he feels the noose tightening,
Jonathan manages to relax a little. Conversely,
Dracula seems keyed up and anxious to be off.

JONATHAN   That's very kind of you, Count.
                        Not to worry. I can kill an
                        hour or two listening to music.

With a curt nod Dracula is gone, leaving Jonathan to sink into an easy chair and listen to the music. But only for a moment. Directly the footsteps of the Count have died away, Jonathan is on his feet and after snatching up a sharp paper knife, which resembles more a stiletto, leaves the room through another door.

INT. GREAT HALL. DAY.

JONATHAN tiptoes across the deserted entrance hall towards the massive front doors which he proceeds cautiously to open. Barely has the gap widened an inch than an ugly grey snout inserts itself with a ferocious snarl. Growls follow as if an entire wolf pack is waiting outside to tear Jonathan to pieces. With a mighty effort he hurls himself against the door to withhold the pressure from without and with a supreme effort manages at last to close it, shooting the bolt for good measure. Breathless, he leans against it for a moment stricken by the fact that he is a doomed man.

INT. BEARDSLEY ROOM. DAY.

JONATHAN enters the room determined to escape and makes straight for the window.

JONATHAN'S POINT OF VIEW:

A drop of two-hundred feet leads to the road and freedom, but various roofs, gutters and buttresses offer a staircase of sorts, albeit a dangerous one where one false step means death.

RESUME BEDROOM:

JONATHAN decides to risk it and eases himself gingerly over the sill.

EXT. CASTLE. DAY.

Precariously, JONATHAN starts his dizzy descent. After negotiating the narrow ledge he drops onto a shallow roof and slides down over the edge till his hands make contact with the guttering. Inching his way along to a drainpipe, he climbs down to a tiny flat roof. The next stage in his escape entails a leap across a gap onto a parapet - this seems almost impossible. But there is no turning back, try he must. Pressing himself against the wall he runs with all his might and launches himself into space. His hands grip the parapet but slip and slip until he is dropping through space, hitting a sloping roof and sliding towards a skylight.

INT. CHAPEL. DAY.

JONATHAN crashes through the glass and falls a short drop into the organ loft where a baroque organ is apparently being played by a ghost. On closer inspection, as he brushes himself off, Jonathan sees that the organ playing a gentle Bach Chorale is functioning by mechanical, not supernatural, means.

INT. CHAPEL DOOR. DAY.

By the eerie light filtering through the crimson stained glass windows set in the outside wall, JONATHAN is able to take in the strange nature of this secret spot. In place of the usual cross a lifelike carving of a giant heart surrounded by a circle of tusks seems to float above the altar which is flanked not by statues of saints but by models of the chemical structure of blood, blown up to resemble modern sculptures. Dominating this shrine dedicated to the Glory of Blood is a mural showing Dracula in medieval robes seated at a banqueting table enjoying a glass of Bull's Blood surrounded by a forest of stakes on which men, women and children suffer a multitude of slow, painful deaths. Attending him are three beautiful women bearing an uncanny likeness to the vampires of the previous night. Other paintings adorning the walls show Dracula in a variety of regal historical costumes ranging from medieval times to the 20th Century. Though his mode of dress changes with the times, Dracula, like Dorian Gray, remains forever young.

Jonathan's first impulse is to flee this temple of eternal youth but, as he descends the stairs to the aisle, he is arrested in his flight by the sight of an open trap door leading to the crypt. Now curiosity overcomes fear and impels him to peer down into the gloom below.

JONATHAN'S POINT OF VIEW:

At the bottom of a flight of steps rests an open casket and in it lies DRACULA apparently asleep. Taking the sturdy paper knife from his jacket pocket, and barely daring to breathe, Jonathan creeps silently down towards him.

INT. CRYPT. DAY.

Ribbons of light from slits in the outside wall illuminate a strange setting for the dormant Count. A large variety of wooden boxes, all big enough to hold a recumbent figure, are stacked amidst piles of earth excavated from the floor itself which is a mass of rubble. Some of the boxes are open and filled with freshly dug earth. On such a bed of clay lies DRACULA, his eyes wide open and stony, his face motionless, set in a mocking smile. Sweat pours from Jonathan's brow as he summons up strength to commit murder. Gripping the knife firmly in his hands Jonathan raises it, trembling, above his head and with all his force plunges the blade into Dracula's chest. A grin of malice passes over Dracula's face as he reaches to take the knife from his chest and slowly withdraws it, dripping gore. Jonathan is transfixed in horror at the failure of his lethal blow. Dracula's eyes stare with hate as he raises the dripping blade and plunges it towards Jonathan's throat. But Jonathan leaps back in time to sustain nothing worse than a gashed cheekbone.
Simultaneously, the door at the far end of the crypt is flung open admitting a BAND OF GYPSIES. Instantly, Jonathan runs up the stairs to the chapel spurred on by their cries of alarm.

INT. CHAPEL. DAY.

Slamming the trap door behind him, Jonathan covers
it with a heavy pew which requires all his strength
to drag into place. Then to the sound of hammering
and muffled shouts, he runs out of the door with all
speed, locking it behind him.

INT. CASTLE CORRIDOR. DUSK.

Outside the chapel door, Jonathan finds himself on
a spiral staircase leading up to a door, which he
discovers to be locked and down to ... the unknown.
He has no choice but to descend.

INT. VAULT. DUSK.

JONATHAN pushes a door open to find himself in a bare
cellar with iron grills set in the wall about sev-
en feet from the ground, giving onto the courtyard
where a good deal of activity sounds to be in progress. Gripping hold of the ledge, Jonathan manages
to haul himself up sufficiently to peer through the
grill.

JONATHAN'S POINT OF VIEW:

EXT. COURTYARD. DUSK.

Two large carts are being loaded with the boxes from
the crypt, which are now all sealed and judging from
the exertions of the gypsies, loaded with earth.
Even as he watches, the leading cart pulls away
through the gateway and over the drawbridge escorted
by Gypsy Bandits on wild ponies.

RESUME:

INT. VAULT. DUSK.

JONATHAN releases his grip, drops to the floor and
makes for the door leading to the spiral staircase.
It has apparently shut itself. Despite all his efforts
it refuses to budge. Instead, another door opens in
the far wall revealing the THREE VAMPIRE GIRLS in
their flowing robes beckoning Jonathan toward their

hungry embrace. Almost in a trance, Jonathan moves towards them like a willing victim. The vampires smile in lustful anticipation and reveal their pointed teeth eager to sink once more into human flesh.
But their smiles vanish as Jonathan kicks one in the stomach with all his force, and delivers a powerful swinging punch to the jaw of another. An even bigger surprise follows as Jonathan is sent flying through the air to land in a heap in the corner. Not only are the vampires unharmed, but their m monstrous strength had proved more than a match for a mere human. As they begin to move in for the kill, Jonathan's next action is one of a desperate man. Taking the rosary from his neck, he wraps it round his fist like a knuckle-duster and leaps up at the foremost vampire. WHACK! This time the connection is holy and the monster crashes into her companion spitting blood and broken teeth. By the time they have recovered, Jonathan has hung the crucifix in the doorway of their room and entered it, leaving the holy talisman of faith to hang like a shield between himself and the cheated vampires.

INT. VAMPIRE LAIR. DUSK

Pictures and sculptures glorifying love decorate this amazing grotto inset with precious stones glittering in the candle-light. But all this is merely a setting for the bizarre collection of lovers sitting on thrones, reclining on cushions, or merely propped against the walls. Lovers in peasant costumes and in uniforms of soldiers, statesmen, kings and emperors attired in styles ranging over a period of 500 years, all dead, sucked dry, withered and mummified. Jonathan takes in this macabre museum to dead love with one horrified glance. His prime concern is to escape and to that end he runs towards a partially open door leading to the failing daylight. He throws it open and almost steps into space. Beneath him is a drop of several hundred feet into the swirling river. Behind him, the uncertain terrors of the howling vampires. Before him, possibly a broken neck, possibly escape. He jumps; and plummets into the river. Widening circles mark his point of disappearance.

DISSOLVE TO: THE DRACULA COAT OF ARMS.

As it recedes from CAMERA it becomes clear that we have been observing a stencil on Dracula's casket being lifted high in the air.

CUT BACK TO REVEAL:

EXT. PORT OF VARNA. DAY

A steam ship of some five thousand tons is loading cargo, including Dracula's consignment of boxes. As the last one is hoisted aboard and lowered into the hold the BOATSWAIN signs a receipt watched by the GYPSY DRIVER.

BOATSWAIN   Received: Fifty crates o' clay
               exported Varna to the port
               of Southampton, England. As
               if there weren't enough there
               already. Talk about carrying
               coals to Newcastle. There
               you are, Dad, back to your
               crystal ball.

He hands the uncomprehending gypsy the receipt, then runs up the gangplank as the carts rumble off along the quayside.

INSERT: close shot: The Ship's Hooter sounding two blasts. Steam fills the frame.

DISSOLVE TO: INSERT:

Close shot: Safety Match Box decorated with a ship and the legend "England's Glory". A loud buzzing like an electric chainsaw comes from within. A hand enters the shot and lifts the box out of frame.

CUT BACK TO REVEAL:

INT. PADDED CELL. DAY.

A plain room with a bed fixed firmly to the wall, a barred window and a heavy metal door with peephole, and a matchbox full of flies, is the world of MORRIS RENFIELD: madman. Covering the gap with his thumb, so as to prevent a mass exodus, Renfield manages to extract a fat, juicy house fly which he surveys hungrily before popping it into his mouth, grating it between his gums with relish.

INSERT: close shot: an eye at the peephole.

CUT TO:

INT. SANATORIUM. DAY.

Cold and austere with doors giving onto private wards from one of which is heard the moans of a dying man. In the foreground observing RENFIELD through a peephole in the cell door is the beautiful but doomed young opera star, LUCIA WEBER. Standing beside her is a clean cut, distinguished-looking man a few years her junior. This is DR. MARTIN SEWARD, her physician whose duty towards her as a patient is complicated by the fact that he is in love with her. Lucy loves him in return but is also susceptible to admirers who make her forget her condition. Lucy turns towards him with a little shudder.

LUCY   He's eating flies.

Dr. Seward observes Renfield through the peephole and addresses him through a small metallic grill.

DR. SEWARD   Why have you taken to consuming flies,
              Renfield?

Renfield, caught in the act, spins round and treats the doctor to a placating smile.

RENFIELD   Because they are very wholesome,
              Doctor Seward. They are life,
              strong life, and give life to me.

DR. SEWARD   They harbour disease, Renfield,
              you must dispose of them.

RENFIELD   Yes, Doctor Seward, certainly,
              I will crush the life out of
              them here and now if you wish,
              but if you could allow me a
              little while longer I shall

47

dispose of them to greater
purpose.

CLOSE SHOT: Dr. Seward's eye through the peephole.

DR. SEWARD (voice-over) I will consider it, Renfield.

DR. SEWARD'S POINT OF VIEW:

RENFIELD nods thankfully then busies himself staring
into the corners of the room.

INT. SANATORIUM CORRIDOR. DAY.

DR SEWARD turns away and speaks to LUCY.

DR. SEWARD   His case grows more interesting
daily. This zoophagous tendency
is a completely new departure.

LUCY   Zoo ... what?

DR. SEWARD   Zoophagous - life-consuming -

LUCY   Well, if nothing else flies
(lightly)   are a very economical diet.
At this rate you'll soon be
able to afford central heating.

DR. SEWARD (showing concern) Are you cold, dearest?

LUCY (wondering if it is the hand of Death
she is feeling) Yes. It is cold
in here, isn't it?

DR. SEWARD (playing along) Now you mention it,
yes. Come along.

Lucy realises he is humouring her and becomes stubborn.

LUCY   First tell me about the patient.
What's a madman doing in your
home for incurables?

Dr Seward, seeing her growing anxiety, reluctantly
informs her.

48

DR. SEWARD   His name is Renfield. Like you
              he was suffering from leukemia.

LUCY   ... Was?

Dr. Seward mentally bites his tongue, evades her
question and hurriedly continues.

DR. SEWARD   He went off to Europe looking
              for a miracle cure and came
              back from Transylvania totally
              deranged.

LUCY (persisting) ... and totally alive.
              How long ago?

DR. SEWARD (reluctantly) About six months, but he's -

To Lucy at death's door, six months seems an eternity.

LUCY (interrupting) A lifetime! Maybe I should
              follow his example? Better mad
              than dead.

Lucy turns back to the peephole and stares at Renfield
with new interest as he commences to prophesize.

RENFIELD   And he shall come riding in
              triumph on the crest of the
              wave. And he will bring to
              the faithful the kiss of peace
              which is life eternal, for
              the blood the life, the power,
              and the glory, amen.

RESUME: CORRIDOR.

DR SEWARD gently pulls LUCY away from the peephole
to face him.

DR. SEWARD   Lucy, come away, please;
              Renfield cannot help us.
              You're upsetting yourself.

LUCY (breaking down) I'm sorry, it's my fault.
              I made you show me around.

                    I thought that seeing other
                    condemned unfortunates like
                    myself would help ... but
                    it doesn't.

DR. SEWARD   Let me see you home.

LUCY (flaring up) Just because I am dying
                    doesn't mean you have to spend
                    every minute with me -
              (she regrets her outburst and softens)
                    No, darling, I've wasted enough
                    of your time as it is. I came here
                    uninvited; it was foolish of me.
                    I can drive myself back.

Dr. Seward looks at her adoringly and takes her hand.

DR. SEWARD   Then I shall call on you tomorrow
                    as usual.

LUCY (falling against his chest weeping) Oh Martin,
                    I'm so afraid. The farewell performance
                    - I can't do it, I can't.

DR. SEWARD (interrupting gently but firmly)
                    You must, Lucy dearest, you must
                    carry on as if you were going to
                    sing forever. You must be strong
                    for all those that care for you
                    and love you; and for me.

She embraces Dr. Seward and kisses him passionate-
ly, then runs off along the gloomy corridor in tears.
Briefly, Dr. Seward goes to follow her, but checks
himself, believing it best not to be witness to her
distress. As her sobbing dies away he turns back to
Renfield's cell.

DR. SEWARD   You have forty-eight hours to
                    get rid of the flies, Renfield.

RESUME: RENFIELD'S CELL.

RENFIELD is standing on his table staring at a corner
of the ceiling.

50

RENFIELD   Thank you, Doctor, you are most
                  kind; almost as kind as the Master.

SLOW DISSOLVE:

THE SS DEMETER Steaming through calm seas at dusk.

SUPERIMPOSE: a pair of burning eyes.

FADE OUT THE SHIP: leaving the eyes alone which are
now seen to be peering from a narrow slit in the
raised lid of the casket containing Dracula!

INT. THE HOLD OF THE SS DEMETER. DUSK.

On ascertaining that he is alone, DRACULA throws
back the lid of the casket, climbs out and begins
to scale a ladder towards an open hatchway in the
deck above.

DISSOLVE TO:

A Death's Head Spider climbing up its web.

CUT BACK TO REVEAL:

INT. RENFIELD'S CELL. DUSK.

RENFIELD, with a childlike smile on his face, watches the climbing spider until a well-known voice
causes him to spin round to the door with a guilty look.

CLOSE UP: DR. SEWARD'S eye looking through the peephole.

DR. SEWARD'S VOICE Show me your matchbox, Renfield.

Sheepishly, Renfield complies and a nest of spiders
cascades onto the floor. Instantly he is on his hands
and knees desperately trying to retrieve them.

DR. SEWARD'S VOICE They are a source of anxiety,
                   Renfield. For your own peace of
                   mind you must get rid of them.

Renfield continues chasing the spiders while jabbering
away to the doctor.

RENFIELD   I was just doing as you said
                  Doctor, disposing of the flies.

DR. SEWARD'S VOICE You need more therapeutic pursuits,
                  Renfield; I shall see to it.

RENFIELD   Thank you, Doctor. Of course,
                  if I might have just a little
                  time longer to clear them out ...

DR. SEWARD'S VOICE Of course, Renfield.

RENFIELD   Thank you, Doctor, thank you!

As Renfield scuttles about the floor the CAMERA zooms into the Death's Head Spider sucking the blood of a fly entangled in its web.

DISSOLVE TO:

What at first appears to be a close shot of the web but which is revealed to be the mesh of a hammock in the boatswain's cabin on board -

THE SS DEMETER. NIGHT.

The BOATSWAIN sleeps blissfully as DRACULA sucks gently from a wound in his neck draining his very life blood, then creeps away like a spider bloated with the blood of a fly, spun in a web of death.

INT. RENFIELD'S CELL. NIGHT.

By the light of the moon, RENFIELD is seen at his barred window feverishly making a primitive cage from rushes and twine.

DISSOLVE TO:

A sparrow pecking up bread on a window-sill. Suddenly a hand enters frame and grabs it away.

INT. RENFIELD'S CELL. DAY.

Renfield stuffs the bird into his home-made cage and laughs in triumph.

Close shot - The bird twittering noisily
Close shot - A seagull screeching
Close shot - A corpse bound in the Union flag
        hitting the water.

EXT. SS. DEMETER. DAY.

The CAPTAIN and CREW, EIGHT MEN in all,stand solemnly
by the rail, heads bowed in remembrance of their
dead shipmate.

CAPTAIN   May his soul rest in peace.

As the seagulls cry mockingly, the CAPTAIN stomps
off to the bridge.

CAPTAIN   Carry on, Mister Mate.

The Mate turns towards the troubled crew.

MATE   Return to your duties!

The men shift and murmur uneasily.

MATE   Come on, jump to it!

Unable to put into words their disquiet, the men
reluctantly disperse.

INSERT: Dr. Seward's eyes staring through the peephole.

DR. SEWARD'S VOICE Have you disposed of the spiders,
        Renfield?

INT, RENFIELD'S CELL. DAY.

RENFIELD turns quickly away from his barred window
and scooping up the matchbox from the cell, bounds over
to the door as pleased as a puppy doing a trick for
its master. He slowly opens the matchbox. It is empty.

DR. SEWARD'S VOICE Well done, Renfield ...

Renfield beams with delight. Renfield runs to his bed
and returns with a framework of a fruit basket which
he proudly holds up for inspection. When the Doctor

speaks again, after a moment's pause, Renfield is taken by surprise.

DR. SEWARD'S VOICE Is that the song of a thrush, Renfield, or a sparrow?

After a moment's hesitation, Renfield runs to the cell window and peers out.

RENFIELD   Both, Doctor, though I fancy the sparrow is closer.

DR. SEWARD'S VOICE Show me what you have made with the remainder of your rushes and twine, Renfield.

Caught out, Renfield reluctantly takes from beneath his bed the caged bird which he brings towards the peephole for the Doctor's inspection.

RENFIELD   I was keeping it as a surprise - for your birthday, Doctor.

DR. SEWARD'S VOICE My first action on receiving such a gift, Renfield, would be to release it. You must do likewise. Renfield breaks down.

RENFIELD   Oh please, Doctor, not yet, not yet a while. I must have a pet of some kind. A little kitten perhaps? There's no harm in that. A nice little sleek playful kitten that I can play with and teach and feed, and feed, and feed!

DR. SEWARD'S VOICE Would you not rather have a cat?

RENFIELD   Oh yes, I would like a cat! I only asked for a kitten lest you should refuse me a cat. No one would refuse me a kitten, would they?

DR. SEWARD'S VOICE At present that is not possible, Renfield, but we shall see.

Renfield's face falls, becomes dangerous, homicidal.

Close shot - An inverted eye.

CUT BACK TO REVEAL:

The inverted head of a dead SAILOR lying on top of a hatch aboard -

THE SS DEMETER. NIGHT.

Fellow members of the CREW stand by holding lanterns and staring with dismay at the dead man; the CAPTAIN kneels at his side and is about to cover him with a tarpaulin when something causes him to freeze. Drops of blood are dripping from the sky onto the dead man's face. Slowly the Captain looks up to where all eyes are now staring in horror. Hanging upside down on the cross tree at the masthead, bloated like some hellish bat, hangs the cloaked figure of DRACULA. Blood trickles over his sharp teeth and drips from his open mouth set in a smile of satisfaction.

JUMP CUT: RENFIELD'S crazed face, blood and feathers in and around his mouth.

INT. RENFIELD'S CELL. NIGHT.

TWO MEDICAL ORDERLIES force RENFIELD into a strait-jacket as DR. SEWARD plunges a hypodermic in his arm.

EXT. SOUTHAMPTON WATER. DAY.

The SS DEMETER steams over the horizon towards CAMERA.

SUPERIMPOSE: Dracula's eyes as the CAMERA cranes down to reveal LUCY idly watching its approach as she speculates on the closing chapter of her brief life.

LUCY   Who shall I take as my last
              lover - who will he be? ...

FADE OUT Dracula's eyes which have appeared to be burning right through her.

LUCY   ... I just can't choose between
                the kind doctor who will fortify
                me or the crazy cowboy who will
                make me forget ...

She smiles forlornly past CAMERA at her unseen companion and, assuming a phony Texan accent, caricatures
her American admirer.

LUCY   ... "Miss Lucy, ah know ah ain't
                good enough to turn the pages of
                yur song sheets but ah jes' know
                you got the sweetes' li'l ole voice
                this side o' heaven."
            (she becomes serious for a moment
            and speaks naturally)
                "Bad mark there, Quincey my boy,
                to mention heaven..."
            (then forces gaiety back into her voice
            as he resumes the imitation)
                ... "But if you jes' hitch
                up along side o' me, we'll
                have ourselves one helluva
                fine ride, drivin' along in
                double harness...

She breaks into a real laugh in which she is joined
by her companion and secretary, MINA MURRAY, who
walks into frame and puts her arm around Lucy's
waist and kisses her affectionately on the cheek.

MINA   Sounds vaguely indecent to me.
                (becoming a little more serious)
                Oh, I don't know; I'm afraid
                I can't help you, Lucy. It's
                nice to have a choice.

MINA, an attractive girl in her mid-twenties, enjoys
a special relationship with Lucy, being as reliable
a friend as she is a secretary.

LUCY   Oh come now, if you were in
                my shoes you'd still marry
                your lovely Jonathan.

MINA (joking) If he doesn't leave me in the
lurch waiting at the church.

LUCY   You were expecting him back
            yesterday, weren't you?

Nina shrugs and smiles though it is plain to see she
is a little worried.

MINA   You know what these business
            trips are ...

LUCY (archly) Yes, well, we needn't go into that.
     (banteringly) He simply must come back.
            He can't afford to disappoint
            the chief bridesmaid. This
            afternoon we're going to select
            my dress. Do you see me in *Eau de Nile*?
            It's very fashionable this year,
            though it rather depends on what
            colour you've chosen for yourself.

MINA (dryly) I rather thought I'd be in white.

Both girls laugh at Lucy's faux-pas. There is obviously
an unspoken pact between them to treat life as a joke.

LUCY   And which of my suitors are we
            meeting at the bandstand, today?
            The poor psychiatrist or the
            crazy cowboy?

MINA (consulting a small diary) Well, according
            to your appointments diary ...
            (flatly) ... both!

They laugh again until Lucy abruptly sobers up.

LUCY   Isn't that ship cutting it a little fine?

Mina turns in time to see the SS DEMETER speeding
full speed ahead toward the narrow harbour entrance,
only a few paces from where they are standing.

MINA   The crew must be blind -
            She's going to collide!

Quicker than it takes to tell, the SS DEMETER is
upon them and with a prolonged screech the ship
scrapes the full length of her hull against the
end of the stone jetty causing them to jump back
with the shock. Another moment and the vessel has
ploughed her way into the waters of the harbour and
through a luckless fishing boat which was too slow in
clearing her path. Meanwhile, the girls recovering
from their initial shock are running along the quayside following the ship's course of destruction.

EXT. SOUTHAMPTON PIER. BANDSTAND. DAY.

The BANDMASTER, conducting his PLAYERS through
Strauss' Die Fledermaus Overture, cannot believe
his eyes as he sees the SS DEMETER steaming straight
towards the pier on which he is giving an afternoon
concert to a jolly THRONG OF HOLIDAY MAKERS. But the
screams of women and cries of children soon convince
him that this is no dream. One by one the band stop
playing to follow his terrified stare at the mountain
of steel rushing toward them, belching forth clouds
of black smoke like an angry volcano. The crash when
it comes is a cacophony of human shrieks and exploding timber made all the more horrific by the dense
smoke which envelops everything in a funereal pall.

JUMP CUT:

MINA and LUCY arrive on the scene to find several
POLICEMEN restoring order, some STRETCHER-BEARERS
carrying away those wounded by falling stanchions,
and others throwing lines to people in the water.
Near the bows of the ship, which is stuck fast in
the pier, they come upon DR. SEWARD setting a broken
leg with an improvised splint close by a tall, lanky
American, QUINCEY MORRIS, who is arguing with a gruff
bearded individual in vague nautical attire.

HARBOURMASTER As Harbourmaster of this here
                Port of Southampton, it is my
                prerogative, if she has been
                abandoned as seems the case,
                to claim this here vessel
                as salvage.

QUINCEY   Then pray, get aboard pronto, sir, or
                 there won't be anything to salvage.

HARBOURMASTER I fail to perceive your meaning, sir.

QUINCEY   The engines are still turning at
                 full speed and unless someone gets
                 their tail on board and does
                 something about it, we'll all be
                 blown to hell and high water.

The Harbourmaster looks worried but holds his ground.

HARBOURMASTER I've sent for a gangplank,
                 now please stand aside sir;
                 it will be here momently.

QUINCEY   Momently is too late!

Snatching a coil of rope, he fashions it into a lariat
and lassoes the flagpole at the bow and hauls himself
aboard before anyone can stop him. The Harbourmaster
is furious but Lucy applauds excitedly and turns to
Mina who is also thrilled by the Texan's daring.

LUCY   Oh Mina, isn't he splendid?
                 Just look at that!
                 (shouting) Bravo, Quincey, Bravo!

Catching sight of Lucy, Quincey smiles a big smile
and waves his cowboy hat before running aft.

LUCY (smitten) As brave as Doug Fairbanks!

Mina is impressed too, but equally aware of the virtues
of Dr. Seward.

MINA   You're lucky in both your
                 boyfriends, Lucy.

She goes to help Dr. Seward tie his improvised splint.
Not wishing to be left out Lucy joins her just as the
gangplank arrives, supervised by a POLICEMAN.

HARBOURMASTER Stay on duty here, Constable, and
                 make sure you let no one on board.

POLICEMAN (darkly) What about the Doctor here,
                    Sir? You never know...

The Harbourmaster stops in his tracks, glances at
the deserted ship and nods approval.

HARBOURMASTER Doctor, you'd best come along as well.
                    This could be a case for quarantine.

DR. SEWARD   I'll be right with you.

So saying he relinquishes his patient to a COUPLE
OF AMBULANCE MEN and makes his way to the gangway
followed by the two girls who are stopped by the
Policeman.

POLICEMAN   I'm sorry ladies - no sightseers.

Lucy becomes petulant.

LUCY   Oh really, Constable, we only ..

MINA uses guile.

MINA (interrupting) We are both qualified nursing
                    sisters, Officer, as Dr. Seward
                    will testify.

The Policeman looks questioningly at Dr. Seward who
nods approval.

DR. SEWARD   That's quite in order, Constable.

The next moment they are climbing the steep gangway
towards the deck as the engines grind to a halt.

INT. SS DEMETER. CREW'S QUARTERS. DAY.

QUINCEY pokes his head around various doors to find
nothing but a deserted ship until the sound of move-
ment from a cabin causes him to draw a Colt revolver
from his belt and approach with caution. Kicking the
door open, he jumps inside, gun at the ready ...
Nothing except for the ship's cat, a sinister black
animal who bristles at Quincey who frowns, slips the
gun away and makes for the topdeck.

DR. SEWARD   Oh, I'm sorry, excuse me.

QUINCEY (simultaneously) Pardon me, Sir, after you.

LUCY brushes between them dispensing introductions as she goes.

LUCY   Dr. Seward, Mr. Morris, Quincey,
              Martin ...

By the time the men have shaken hands watched by an amused Mina, Lucy has reached the top of the companion-way where a strange sight greets her.

INT. BRIDGE. DAY.

INSERT: A crucifix entwined in rosary beads clasped in praying hands held fast by rigor mortis.

ZOOM BACK to reveal THE CAPTAIN, his face set in a terrified grimace, lashed to the wheel. DR. SEWARD rushes forward to examine him followed by the others watched by BLACK CAT who seems to be trailing QUINCEY.

QUINCEY   How long has he been gone?

DR. SEWARD   Several hours at least.

LUCY   Then how did he steer the ship?

QUINCEY   I reckon someone else did the steering.

LUCY   Then they're still aboard.

This observation gives pause for thought, until...

MINA   Look at this, the pages of the
              entire voyage have been torn
              from the log.

Mina offers up the ripped log book in evidence.

DR. SEWARD   This has all the signs of mutiny.

QUINCEY   Mutiny without a crew? T'weren't
              as much as a mouse down below.

Let's see what the Harbourmaster
comes up with.

THE DECK OF THE SS DEMETER:

HARBOURMASTER Not a soul. I've searched the
whole ship from stem to stern -
everywhere but the hold.

QUINCEY   Right, I'll take care of that.
Doc's up on the bridge with
the corpses - best you give
him a hand.

The Harbourmaster blanches.

HARBOURMASTER Well, I don't know ...

QUINCEY (briskly) Look sailor, as first man
on board I claim this vessel as
salvage and accordingly take
command, so either jump to it,
or jump off!

As the Harbourmaster hurries off he almost bumps into
the TWO GIRLS about to take their leave.

LUCY   I'd love to join the manhunt,
Quincey, but I really must be
off to the theatre. You are
coming tonight?

QUINCEY   Wild horses couldn't keep me
away, Lucy.

He takes his hat off and kisses her on the mouth, an
action noticed by Dr. Seward with a pang of jealousy
from his vantage point on the Bridge.

QUINCEY   ... and all the luck in the world.

LUCY   Thank you, darling, see you later.

MINA   Your tickets will be at the
box office and don't forget
the party at Lucy's afterwards.

QUINCEY (winking) Yer darn tootin' honey.

As he makes his way towards the hold, and the girls head for the gangway, Lucy blows a kiss to Dr. Seward who is carrying the dead body down from the Bridge with the assistance of the Harbourmaster.

LUCY   Till tonight!

As Quincey sees this and the look of admiration in Dr. Seward's eyes, it is his turn to be jealous. Even the ship's cat who continues to follow Quincey around arches its back in protest.

INT. HOLD OF THE SS DEMETER. DAY.

QUINCEY breaks open the lids of the boxes with a crowbar and snorts with disgust at the worthless treasure trove of dirt. Suddenly a figure we recognise as DRACULA is silhouetted in the open hatchway above.

DRACULA   You will derive little profit
              from fifty boxes of clay, sir.
              I am the customer to whom they
              are consigned. May I take them
              off your hands?

Quincey looks up and wipes the sweat from his brow.

QUINCEY   Fifty boxes of gosh darn dirt!

He laughs to himself and shouts up to Dracula.

QUINCEY   It's all yours, partner, take
              it away. I've still got plenty
              reason to celebrate.

He lets out a great whoop of joy at his salvage prize as the hatch covers come off in a blaze of light.

THE GRAND THEATRE, SOUTHAMPTON, NIGHT.

From his armchair in the Royal Box, QUINCEY, as elegantly dressed as any member of the smart audience beneath him, sips iced champagne and listen entranced to LUCY'S golden voice soaring magically from the brilliantly lit stage on which she is giving the performance of her life as Joan of Arc in Tchaikovksy's Opera, *Maid of Orleans*.

From his seat in the front row of the stalls, DR. SEWARD also watches, fighting a losing battle to hold back the tears. In the wings, MINA too is carried away by the pathos of the moment. Lucy being the focus of her attention, she is unaware of a cloaked figure watching from the shadows in the wings opposite. But not so Lucy. As she is dragged by her captors to the stake close to where he is standing, she gives a start of recognition at the imposing sight of DRACULA haloed in the glow of a score of spotlights. He too is transported by Lucy's song which reaches its climax as she is engulfed in shimmering flame. Waves of tumultuous applause drown the orchestral finale as the stage is deluged with flowers. Lucy bows to all corners of the auditorium, then smiles at Quincey and Dr. Seward who are on their feet frantically applauding with everyone else. But of the mysterious stranger there is no sign. Lucy gives a tiny frown of disappointment before smiling once again to her public as the ovation continues.

EXT. LUCY'S ESTATE. NIGHT.

An elegant floodlit mansion forms a picturesque backdrop to the dancing COUPLES and jazzing BAND which are the centre of Lucy's midnight garden party. Elsewhere, the GUESTS stroll among the statues strung with Chinese lanterns or smooch in the shadows of the towering trees. From the dark recesses of a rose bower, DRACULA looks through a pair of opera glasses at LUCY dancing a slow rag with DR. SEWARD.

From Dracula's close-up POINT OF VIEW, it is easy to guess that Dr. Seward is proposing to Lucy, even though we are too far off to hear the words, and that she is responding sympathetically. Suddenly the binoculars sweep through the dancing crowd until they find QUINCEY whispering to the BAND LEADER and slipping him a pound note. That does the trick, and soon the maestro is leading his boys into a jazzed up square dance. Now the binoculars follow the grinning Quincey onto the floor where everyone is at a loss as how best to cope with this new crazy rhythm. Not so Quincey, who takes Lucy away from Dr. Seward with a cheeky bow, and leads her into a hilarious conglomeration of Charleston-cum-Hoedown. Dr. Seward showing a mixture of anger and concern falls back with the rest of the crowd to watch the cavorting couple go through their expertly-improvised paces. And though Lucy soon begins to tire she becomes furious when Dr. Seward orders the band leader to stop. Some of the onlookers are puzzled while others seem to guess the reason for the termination of the strenuous number. Quincey sees it as a personal challenge, and being somewhat the worse for drink, takes a swing at Dr. Seward and knocks him down. Before Dr. Seward can pick himself up to retaliate Lucy has burst into tears, run off the floor, and disappeared into the darkness before anyone can stop her. An ugly scene is averted by the band leader who swings the orchestra into the Black Bottom which sets everyone dancing again - except for Quincey and Dr. Seward who glare furiously at each other across the dance floor.

Lucy's flight takes her close to Dracula's hidden vantage point where MINA, who has followed her from a discreet distance, catches up with her.

MINA   Do forgive them, Lucy.
            The Doctor was only acting for
            the best, and Quincey was too drunk
            to know better!

LUCY (bitterly) Well I'd rather drop dead
            dancing than be buried in
            that dreadful sanatorium.

MINA (placatingly) Come back and have a nice
            quiet drink with them.

Lucy rounds on her.

LUCY   And stop treating me like an ...
            (she is going to say 'invalid')
            ... you're my secretary, not a
            paid nurse; now leave me!

MINA (hurt)   Shall I bring your mail up to your
                 room with breakfast, as usual?

LUCY (angrily) Yes, yes, yes, together with
                 the pills, and the medicine,
                 and all the other rubbish.

Lucy hurries off into the depths of the garden, wishing to
be alone in her misery, leaving Mina to walk off sadly.

A FLOODLIT FOUNTAIN. NIGHT.

A tear trickles down LUCY'S cheek as she contem-
plates the deep dark waters and the oblivion they
offer. Even her reflection seems to be beckoning. She
is literally on the brink of suicide when she feels
a pair of hands on her shoulders turning her around
to face a tall dark stranger who cups her face in
his hands.

DRACULA (gently) I would much prefer to remember
                 you as Joan of Arc than Ophelia.

Lucy responds to him almost like a lover in a dream
and looks at him curiously without fear.

DRACULA   Do you know me?

LUCY (falteringly) Yes and no; not your name,
                 but I have seen you before.

Dracula too has fond memories.

DRACULA   ... in Paris, Berlin, Milan, Budapest ...

To Lucy it is like a dream come true.

LUCY   I would see you across the
                 footlights. You were always
                 close to me, but never as close
                 as tonight.

DRACULA (urgently) I no longer wish to be a
                 spectator. The time has come
                 for me to be part of you.

LUCY (wistfully) I'm afraid you're too late.

DRACULA (firmly) No ... I can save you.

LUCY (hoping against hope) But no one can cure
            leukemia. Are you a specialist?
            Where is your practice?

DRACULA (with a hint of irony)
            I've accomplished some of my
            finest work in Central Europe,
            especially Transylvania...

Lucy draws in a breath recalling the case of Renfield,
but speaks obliquely.

LUCY   You must be a miracle worker.

Dracula continues with growing emotion.

DRACULA   ... I work alone and shun publicity,
                and with the exception of those cases
                I take merely to live, I reserve
                my skill solely for those worth
                saving for their talent alone.
                And were I not pledged to secrecy
                you would know them for the illustrious
                artists they are. But not one of
                them is more worthy of life than
                you - your voice has more colour
                than Turner ever dreamed of,
                there is more music in your every
                movement than in a romance by Sibelius,
                more poetry in your smile than a
                verse of Baudelaire. You are a living
                work of art, complete and eternal -
                how can you die?

Lucy's tears are no tears of joy as she succumbs
totally to Dracula's spell.

LUCY   You are not promising me
                forgetfulness in a dizzy spin,
                neither are you preparing me
                to meet death with fortitude -
                you are giving me life.

DRACULA (whispering) I will be your new lifeblood,
for the blood is the life,
the blood is the life ...

Lucy allows herself to be hypnotised and drawn towards
him. The distant music has turned into a languorous
waltz. Gently she rests her head on Dracula's shoulder,
gently he rocks her in rhythm to the pulsating music.
He caresses her closed eyes, kisses her mouth and
neck. Gently his teeth penetrate her throat and all
the time she is dreamily swaying. As Dracula drinks
her blood she smiles and whispers.

LUCY   Death is departing from me,
                death is draining away,
                draining away, away ...

DISSOLVE to Lucy's Dream:

LUCY is part of the fountain. It has become the
fountain of Eternal Youth, She sings ecstatically in
the sun as the shining water dances off her golden skin.
She is reborn. Somewhere, a long way off, someone
is calling her.

EXT. GARDEN. NIGHT.

MINA is searching for Lucy with a flashlight and
calling her name. Suddenly she sees her, dancing
with closed eyes, alone by the fountain. Mina runs
up and touches her on the shoulder.

MINA   Lucy, it's cold, you must come to bed.

Lucy comes back to reality with a start and looks
about her at a total loss. When she speaks, her
voice is full of regret.

LUCY   My lover, he's gone.

Something flits through the trees and flies off. Mina
puts a shawl around Lucy's shoulders and leads her
towards the house.

MINA   Quincey and the Doctor left
                hours ago. I waited up for you.

LUCY   I feel dizzy, it must be the champagne.

MINA   Stop a moment.

Mina notices two specks of blood on Lucy's neck.

MINA   You must have pricked yourself. There!

She brushes away the blood while Lucy smiles to herself remembering.

LUCY   It is nothing. I was dancing.

MINA   Well next time, don't choose
               a rose bush for a partner.

Arm in arm the two girls walk off towards the darkened house.

EXT. SKY. NIGHT.

A BAT flies past the moon.

EXT. RENFIELD'S CELL. NIGHT.

RENFIELD grips the bars and watches the bat in a fever of religious devotion.

RENFIELD   Long have I prayed for your coming,
               dear Master, and now that you are
               near, I await your commands, and
               you will not pass me by will you,
               dear Master, in your
               distribution of good things?

EXT. SKY. NIGHT.

The BAT circles once as if acknowledging Renfield's prayer and goes out of sight into some nearby trees.

RENFIELD'S VOICE Amen!

EXT. RAILWAY STATION SOUTHAMPTON EAST. DAY.

DR SEWARD is standing on an almost deserted platform staring up the line into the early morning mist, lost in thought, when he recognizes with a start a familiar, if unexpected, voice.

MINA   Dr. Seward! Thank God! What luck!

There, on the opposite platform is MINA looking worried and agitated.

MINA   I tried phoning the sanatorium
                but they said you had already left.

DR. SEWARD   Mina! Good gracious, what on earth
                (alarmed) ... it's not Lucy, is it?

MINA (quickly) She's had a relapse. She
                must be at the sanatorium by
                now. They sent an ambulance.
                When I went into her room
                this morning she ...

The train drowns her explanation and hides her from view as it arrives at her platform. But soon she has boarded the carriage and is shouting to Dr. Seward through the window of her compartment.

MINA   ... I couldn't wake her, not for
                some time anyway, and even then...

DR. SEWARD   What were the symptoms?

MINA (hesitantly) Well, she was weak and feverish,
                and when she tried to get up she
                had a dizzy spell and collapsed
                so I put her back to bed and phoned...

DR. SEWARD (interrupting) Speak up, I can't hear you!

Further speech is rendered impossible by the arrival of the train at Dr. Seward's platform. From one of the carriage windows leans the cloaked figure of a stout old man with a round, cheery face and billowing silver locks. The train brings him into a big CLOSE-UP and halts. It is none other than Dr. Seward's old teacher, Professor VAN HELSING, greeting his ex-pupil with a laugh and a jest.

VAN HELSING   Ah ha! The first sign of
               madness - talking to oneself.
               I always said insanity was
               contagious, remember?

He embraces the slightly distracted Dr. Seward.

VAN HELSING   How are you, my boy?

DR. SEWARD   Very well, Professor. Excuse me!

To Van Helsing's surprise, Dr. Seward shakes himself
off and jumps into the carriage.

INT. COMPARTMENT. DAY.

DR. SEWARD lowers the window and talks across to
MINA in the opposite carriage.

DR. SEWARD   Mina, what is all this about?
               Start from last night.

MINA (flustered) After you'd gone I found her
               in the rose garden. I think
               she'd had a little too much.
               She'd cut herself on one of
               the shrubs - nothing much -
               (she points at her throat)
               Just there. She'd been dancing
               with her lover, she said.

DR. SEWARD (alarmed) Her lover?

Mina knows she is making the case sound totally im-
plausible and finishes off lamely.

MINA   I know it sounds silly - but
               you did ask.

DR. SEWARD (exasperated) Lucy sounds as if
               she's got an almighty hangover,
               and you're acting as if you're still
               tipsy - how, otherwise could you
               have left her alone?

71

MINA (urgently) I didn't leave her until
she was safely in the ambulance
with a nurse. Please, you must
believe me. It's serious.
Jonathan's back home. I have
to see him. His mother telephoned
early this morning - most upset,
she wouldn't say what was wrong,
but ...

The rest of Mina's shouted message is lost in the
cacophony of her departing train. Dr. Seward turns
on hearing Van Helsing's voice.

VAN HELSING Is this how you diagnose all
your patients, my boy; from
a moving train?

And now their train is moving.

DR. SEWARD (apologetically) Oh Professor,
forgive me, please. Are these yours?

EXT. STATION PLATFORM. DAY.

VAN HELSING staggers a little as he lands, but is
saved from falling by DR. SEWARD who is becoming increasingly embarrassed by the indignity he is causing
his esteemed Professor.

DR. SEWARD I am sorry. She's gone
completely scatty.

VAN HELSING Pretty all the same.
(archly)
Pity her Jonathan's come back
so soon.

DR. SEWARD Professor, I hardly know the girl.

VAN HELSING Aha! One of those brief
encounters. What's her name?

DR. SEWARD Mina! I was at a party last
night given by a friend.

VAN HELSING   And you were seeing them off.
               The friend, I did not see ...

DR. SEWARD   By now Lucy should be in
               bed at the sanatorium.

He bites his lip, seeing that he is getting into
deep water and being totally misunderstood by Van
Helsing who starts acting like a Dutch Uncle.

VAN HELSING   Pretty girls, parties in the
               sanatorium all night long.
               You invited your old Professor
               all the way over from Amsterdam
               to play nursemaid to your
               madman, this Renfield, while
               you have a good time, ya?

DR. SEWARD   Lucy is one of my patients,
               Professor, and as for parties
               on the premises, it's simply ...

VAN HELSING   (interrupting with a chuckle)
               I know, I know. Whatever else,
               you could never be guilty of
               misconduct. Not only were you
               my brightest pupil, Martin,
               you were also the least
               frivolous, ya?

A little deflated by Van Helsing's remark, Dr. Seward
nevertheless replies with a wry smile.

DR. SEWARD   Yes, I'm afraid it's still
               the same old "serious Seward".
               It was very good of you to
               come, Professor.

VAN HELSING   Not at all. Your Popsy interests
               me as much as your madmen.

Laughing, Van Helsing takes his arm and hurries him
toward the station exit.

INT. SANATORIUM CORRIDOR. DAY.

Quiet, except for the voice of Renfield singing a hymn, and deserted save for a MALE NURSE pushing a trolley containing a corpse covered with a sheet towards a pair of swing doors at the end of the corridor. As they bump through and disappear from view one of the ward doors opens a little revealing a patient gazing surreptitiously about her. It is LUCY looking very pale and feverish in a nightdress with a chiffon scarf around her throat.
Convinced the coast is clear, she walks unsteadily towards the sound of Renfield's voice. Pausing for breath at his door she whispers urgently through the grill.

LUCY   Renfield, Renfield, quickly,
                I want to speak to you.

Close shot: Peephole: Renfield's eye staring at Lucy.

RENFIELD'S VOICE (accusingly)
                You are the Doctor's girl.

LUCY (protesting) I am nobody's girl.
                But you and I; we share
                something in common.

RENFIELD   Yes, we are patients of Dr. Seward.

LUCY   No, Renfield, we owe our allegiance
                to another master. He who brings
                the kiss of peace which is life
                eternal... Where is he, Renfield?
                     (urgently)
                I must see him, I must.

There is an ominous pause followed by Renfield ranting and raving at the top of his voice.

RENFIELD   All over! All over! He has
                deserted me. There is no
                hope for me, Master. Master,
                why hast thou forsaken me?
                I am doomed. Without the
                blood there is no life.

74

The blood is life, etc.

As Renfield's cries echo down the corridor, Lucy looks around in alarm and not without reason, for already a female NURSE is hurrying around the corner towards her. Lucy panics, and starts running back to her room only to collapse with exhaustion. The worried nurse kneels down and attempts to revive her.

NURSE DANVERS Oh Miss Weber, what are you
                doing out of bed? I said you
                were not to move until you
                had the Doctor's permission.

She is about to drag Lucy back to her room when suddenly DR. SEWARD and VAN HELSING appear, attracted by Renfield's shouts as are TWO MALE NURSES who arrive from the other direction.

DR. SEWARD (furiously to the nurse)
             What is going on, Nurse Danvers?

Without waiting for a reply he turns to the Male Nurses.

DR. SEWARD   Get a stretcher - no don't bother.
              Stay with Professor Van Helsing.
              (to the Professor)
              Renfield's in there, Professor.

VAN HELSING Now is a good time to examine him
             while you take care of your Popsy.

Dr. Seward picks Lucy up in his arms, considerably disturbed by her condition.

DR. SEWARD   Oh Lucy, Oh Lucy, my dear sweet girl.

Nurse Danvers attempts to excuse herself as she leads Dr. Seward towards Lucy's room.

NURSE DANVERS She was sleeping peacefully
                when I left her Dr. Seward.
                I was only...

DR. SEWARD (interrupting) What's her pulse rate?

NURSE DANVERS   Sixty-five, Doctor.

DR. SEWARD   And her temperature?

NURSE DANVERS   Two degrees below normal, Doctor.

Their voices die away as they enter Lucy's room and Van Helsing is admitted to Renfield's cell.

INT. RENFIELD'S CELL. DAY.

As soon as he realizes the presence of authority, Renfield's ravings cease and by the time the Professor enters he is calm and reasonable.

VAN HELSING (affably) Would you like some sugar
            to get your flies round again... ?

RENFIELD (laughing) Not such! Flies are poor things,
            after all!

VAN HELSING   And spiders?

RENFIELD   Blow spiders! What's the use
            of spiders? There isn't anything
            in them to eat or dr...
            (he checks himself on the word
            'drink' which does not go unnoticed)
            ... Chicken-Feed! I'm past all
            that sort of nonsense. You might
            as well ask a man to eat a
            molecule with a pair of
            chopsticks as try to interest me
            in the lesser carnivores when I
            know what is before me.

VAN HELSING (blandly) I see. You want bigger
            things to sink your teeth in.
            How would you like to breakfast
            on an elephant?

RENFIELD (with dignity) Coming from an individual
            who has revolutionized therapeutics
            by his discovery of the continuous
            evolution of brain matter, that
            remark, Professor, is anal.

76

Somewhat put out by Renfield's aplomb, the Professor too, becomes more composed.

VAN HELSING Some people I know fancy that
             life is a positive, perpetual
             entity and that by consuming
             a multitude of live things,
             no matter how low in the
             scale of creation, one might
             indefinitely prolong life.

RENFIELD (calmly) I have no wish to discuss
             metaphysics, Professor. My one
             desire is to leave here at once
             - now - this very hour, this
             very moment if I may.

VAN HELSING Can you tell me frankly your
             reason for wishing to be free?

RENFIELD   If I were free to speak
             I should not hesitate a moment,
             but I am not my own master
             in the matter. I can only
             ask you to trust me. If I am
             refused, the responsibility
             does not rest with me.

VAN HELSING Alas, your petition stands condemned
             out of your own mouth, my friend.

RENFIELD (snapping) Damn all thick-headed Dutchmen!
             Take yourself and your idiotic
             brain theories somewhere else.

VAN HELSING (laughing) Aha! Now that is better.
             You had me worried there,
             momentarily. Later, we
             will meet again and have a
             little dri ...
             (he plays Renfield at his own game)
             ... a little supper, perhaps.

As the Professor goes to leave Renfield grabs hold of him, becoming violent once more.

RENFIELD   I implore you, let me out
                  of this place at once. Send me
                  away how you will and where
                  you will, send keepers with
                  me with whips and chains;
                  let them take me in a
                  strait-jacket, manacled and
                  leg-ironed, even to jail,
                  but let me out of this! You
                  don't know what you do by
                  keeping me here. Their blood
                  will be on your hands.

The Male Nurses pull Renfield away and hurl him into
a corner, then follow the Professor out and lock the
door behind them. A moment later, Renfield is on his
feet hammering against the door and shouting through
the grill.

RENFIELD   Don't you know that I am
                  sane and earnest now, that
                  I am no lunatic in a mad fit,
                  but a sane man fighting for
                  his life. The blood is the
                  life, the blood is the life!
                  Let me go! Let me go!

Impotently, he collapses sobbing to the floor.

INT. LUCY'S WARD. DAY.

Small, white and austere with melancholy windows
looking onto wooded grounds. LUCY lies in bed unconscious, looking deathly pale. The NURSE is helping
DR. SEWARD prepare for a blood transfusion when VAN
HELSING enters.

DR. SEWARD   Thank you, Nurse. I'll
                  ring if I need you.

NURSE   Very well, Doctor. I'll be
                  standing by.

VAN HELSING   The chart, Nurse, please.

She hands the Professor Lucy's chart and leaves the room. Hiding his alarm at what he sees, the Professor sets about restoring Dr. Seward's equanimity as his blood begins to flow in Lucy's veins.

VAN HELSING   Your blood will soon restore
              the roses to her cheeks, my boy.

DR. SEWARD (perplexed) Ha! Roses! I don't
              understand it. Look at that mark on
              her throat. Even if it was caused
              by a thorn how could it account
              for her losing so much blood?

Van Helsing examines the marks on Lucy's throat trying to belie his worst fears.

VAN HELSING   No rose bush it was, certainly.
              The skin around the wound is
              dis-coloured as if something had been...

He discreetly refrains from completing the sentence aloud, and continues his train of thought.

VAN HELSING   ... this Renfield ...

DR. SEWARD (suddenly remembering)
              Oh yes, how did you find Renfield?

VAN HELSING   Blood fixated and desperate for freedom.

DR. SEWARD (puzzled) That's a new development.

VAN HELSING   Your Lucy was collapsed near his
              cell. How well does she know him?

DR. SEWARD   Hardly at all. She accompanied me
              once on my rounds. She heard him
              ranting away and that was about all.

VAN HELSING   Ranting, of what was he ranting?

DR. SEWARD   ... He mentioned 'blood' rather
              a lot I seem to remember, and
              something about the coming of
              the Messiah - Master, the master

79

                    - it's just that he sounded
                    like an Old Testament prophet.

Dr. Seward becomes aware of Van Helsing's growing
discomfort.

DR. SEWARD   Professor, I have known you
                a long time. You have a theory.

VAN HELSING (cautiously) Yes, I have a theory
                but you would not believe it.
                I hardly dare believe it myself.

DR. SEWARD   Something to do with Renfield?

VAN HELSING (passively) Perhaps, indirectly,
                I can't say.
                (snapping out of it)
                I must go to London, now,
                immediately. There are books at
                the University College Hospital
                which I must consult.

Dr. Seward is surprised at Van Helsing's sudden de-
cision but refrains from questioning it.

DR. SEWARD   The duty driver will take
                you to the station. Look,
                I'm afraid I'm causing you
                a lot of inconvenience,
                Professor, and ...

VAN HELSING (indignantly) Since when has saving
                life been an inconvenience?

He begins to disconnect the transfusion equipment.

VAN HELSING (indignantly) Here, that is enough.
                Any more and you will be needing
                a transfusion yourself. Tomorrow
                she will be stronger, you too.
                She will need the utmost care.
                And on no account must these
                windows be left open.
                (he closes a sash window and
                 bends up the catch)

```
DR. SEWARD      I'll have a nurse on
                constant duty.

VAN HELSING     We are the best nurses, you and I.
                Keep watch all night.
                See she is well fed and, hah!
                (smiling) Why do I need to tell
                you what to do - sometimes I still
                imagine you are my pupil.

DR. SEWARD      I rather think I always
                will be, Professor.
```

Van Helsing is moved by the warmth of Seward's voice,
for truth to tell, the older man does have a paternal
regard for the protégé. He replies gruffly to disguise
his feelings.

```
VAN HELSING     Good! Then I can start sending you my
                bill for tuition once again. Tot ziens!
```

With this parting phrase of Dutch he is gone, leaving
Dr. Seward to sink back in his chair and take hold of
Lucy's wrist as much to give her strength as to feel
her pulse.

INT. SANATORIUM. DAY.

The car bearing VAN HELSING to the station sweeps down
the gravelled drive and out of the gates. DRACULA, who
has been following its departure from the depths of the
shrubbery smiles to himself and turns his attention towards
a GARDENER and his BOY clipping a hedge close to the
barred windows of Renfield's cell on the ground floor of
the building.

INT. RENFIELD'S CELL. DAY.

As a click announces the opening of the door and the
arrival of supper, RENFIELD hurls himself at the unsus-
pecting KEEPER, knocking him unconscious to the floor,
and then bounds through the doorway.

INT. LUCY'S WARD. DAY.

DR. SEWARD is leaning over LUCY, with his back to the door, taking her temperature when RENFIELD bursts in to attack her. Overcoming his surprise at finding the Doctor blocking his objective he attempts to hurl him away - but unsuccessfully. The Doctor, despite his loss of blood, is more than a match for Renfield who nevertheless sinks his teeth into the Doctor's wrist before a kick in the groin sends him howling to the floor. Pressing the alarm bell, Dr. Seward half collapses on the bed. Moments later TWO MEDICAL ORDERLIES, also the KEEPER, the STAFF DOCTOR and NURSE DANVERS arrive on the scene.

KEEPER   He's overpowered me,
                Doctor. He's been as good
                as gold lately.

FIRST ORDERLY (simultaneously) His arms, his arms,
                take his arms.

STAFF DOCTOR Dr. Seward, you're hurt. Let me see.

NURSE DANVERS Oh my God, what's happening here?

But Dr. Seward is engrossed in Renfield's strange behaviour.

DR. SEWARD   Don't touch him.

They all stare with varying degrees of disgust as Renfield laps up the blood which has fallen onto the floor from Dr. Seward's wrist.

DR. SEWARD   Go with them, Renfield. Quietly.

The blood has gone. Locked in his own fantasies, Renfield allows himself to be led away peacefully.

RENFIELD (muttering) The blood is the life!
                The blood is the life!

As the Staff Doctor starts to bandage his wrist, Dr. Seward collapses unconscious in his arms. Continuing his first aid, the Staff Doctor gives instructions.

STAFF DOCTOR He's suffering from shock, fetch a trolley.

The ORDERLY runs out.

STAFF DOCTOR Nurse, bring me a strong
                sedative to his room. He'll
                also need stitches, but this
                will do till we get him to bed.

NURSE DANVERS And what about the patient, sir,
                Miss Weber here? As I told you,
                she's an important case.

STAFF DOCTOR My patient is even more
                important. I'll lock her
                in and you can attend to
                her later. Now hurry.

As she hastens out, the trolley arrives and Dr.
Seward is lifted gently aboard and wheeled quickly
from the room. As the key is heard turning in the
lock LUCY opens her eyes, sits up in bed and gazes
through the window to where DRACULA appears silhouetted against a blood red sun setting through the
trees. Smiling he walks towards her while she, in
turn, still weak and shaking, drags herself from the
bed and staggers over to the window. Summoning up all
her strength she tries to lift the sash, unsuccessfully.
Panting with the effort, she slips down the glass and
collapses against it breathing heavily. Collecting
herself she rubs the misted glass and peers out for
her lover. A sigh of regret escapes her lips when
she sees that he is gone.

EXT. RENFIELD'S CELL. DUSK.

The unbreakable glass window is ajar. RENFIELD
stares through the bars directly at CAMERA and
speaks bitterly through the gap.

RENFIELD   I know you wish to enter
                and that you may enter,
                uninvited. It is not to me
                you bring the gift of peace
                but to another. As you deny
                me, so I deny you.

Renfield shuts and fastens the window.

REVERSE ANGLE CUT:

DRACULA looks back at RENFIELD with an enigmatic smile. Behind him the sun has almost set. Slowly, Dracula parts his black cape revealing the GARDEN-ER'S BOY, naked. A mop of golden hair, blue eyes staring blankly from an angelic face with limbs of natural grace all combine to produce a creature of exquisite beauty and innocence. Simply by 'willing it' Dracula causes the hypnotised child to raise its arms. Renfield, staring through the closed window is mystified and growing fearful. Slowly Dracula takes hold of the boy's wrist and with a flick of his sharp thumbnail cuts the vein. As blood pulses from the wound Renfield begins to tremble. Dracula lowers his own arm as the blood trickles down the milk-white arm of the boy. Renfield is fighting a losing battle to suppress his lust for blood.
Dracula calmly awaits the inevitable. With a cry of anguish Renfield opens the window and stretches out towards the blood which is tantalisingly just out of reach. By now Renfield's state is equivalent to that of a pathetic drug addict desperate for a fix. As the sun sinks from sight, the sweating Renfield capitulates and in a dry, tremulous voice, agrees to pay the price.

RENFIELD   Come in, Lord and Master, enter...

An instant later Dracula metamorphoses into a red cloud, the colour of blood. Then as the boy moves a step forward and Renfield snatches his wrist and sucks on it like a parched beast, the cloud of blood rushes in a psychic whirlwind past him into the room and out through the grill in the door.

INT. LUCY'S WARD. DUSK.

To the sound of unearthly music, the cloud of glitter-ing blood whirls beneath the door and changes back into the imposing shape of DRACULA. Like a modern messiah he extends his arms to the incredulous LUCY who drags herself towards him on her knees like a nun at her devotions. As the music rises to a hymn of praise

Dracula unbuttons his shirt and opens an artery in his chest revealing His precious BLOOD. Lucy parts her lips and sensuously covers the wound with her mouth and with closed eyes, drinks. The music shimmers as images float and dissolve until Dracula is drawing blood from Lucy's neck. Their pulses race in unison as the ritual is consummated and the music throbs to a climax.

INT. DR. SEWARD'S BEDROOM. DAY.

A narrow shaft of sunlight beams through a crack in the curtains and falls directly on the face of the sleeping DR. SEWARD. His eyes blink open, dazzled, and a moment later he is out of bed and pulling the curtains on a brilliant sunrise. For a moment he is totally disorientated then remembering the events of yesterday with horror, he quickly slips a dress-ing gown over his pyjamas and hurries from the room.

INT. SANATORIUM CORRIDOR. DAY.

Deeply concerned, DR. SEWARD runs down the corridor and flings open Lucy's door and enters.

INT. LUCY'S WARD. DAY.

The room is deserted. The bed is empty, neat and tidy and newly made up. DR. SEWARD gazes around him uncomprehendingly until a footfall in the corridor fetches him to the door.

INT. CORRIDOR. DAY.

NURSE DANVERS stops in her tracks and looks nervously at DR. SEWARD who speaks to her as if in a dream.

DR. SEWARD   Why have you moved Miss Weber?

Pulling herself together Nurse Danvers speaks as evenly as possible.

NURSE DANVERS Miss Weber died sir,
              at 4:30 this morning.

Dr. Seward acts as if shot.

CUT TO:

INT. THE S.S. DEMETER. DAY.

The ship's cat follows at the heels of QUINCEY who, pleased as punch, strides the deck of his prize packet giving instructions to a DAPPER LITTLE MAN in a bowler hat carrying a large account book.

QUINCEY   ... and I want every single item on board evaluated from the crow's nest right down to the ship's cat.

LITTLE MAN   That will take some little time, Mister Morris. Lloyds of London would be able to give you an immediate estimate, I'm ...

QUINCEY   I want an accurate assessment, sir, not an immediate estimate. If that had been the case I wouldn't have wasted a whole day tracking you down. Now are you the best auctioneers and valuers in these here parts, or are you not?

LITTLE MAN (servile) Indubitably Mr. Morris, and very grateful of your patronage I'm sure. It's just so difficult to know where to make a start.

QUINCEY   Then start at the top and work down, sir.

LITTLE MAN   Even the flags Mr. Morris?

Quincey glances up at the flags indicated by the Little Man.

QUINCEY   Even so ...

Then he does a double take at the four flags flying at the masthead.

QUINCEY   Can you figure out their meanin', sir?

LITTLE MAN (superciliously)
               Only their value, Mr. Morris.

As the Little Man resigns himself to making a start
on the formidable inventory, Quincey makes his way
to the front of the mainmast where is situated the
flag locker, a simple wooden structure of pigeon
holes containing a different flag for each letter of
the alphabet. As he suspected, four flags are missing.
A, C, L and Y. It takes only a second to rearrange
them to read the message flying at the masthead for
all to see. Quincey becomes thoughtful and then annoyed
with himself.

QUINCEY (quietly) C-L-A-Y. Ah' think the Captain
               was tryin' to tell ya' somethin'
               yesterday. Quincey m' boy ...
               (he glances down into the hold)
               But you was too busy lookin'
               down when you should'a been
               a lookin' up.

He looks to the masthead once more where the dead
man's message is triumphantly flying in the wind.

EXT. SOUTHAMPTON QUAYSIDE. DAY.

TWO sweating LABOURERS have paused in their exertions
of loading heavy sacks onto a cart for a word with
QUINCEY who listens attentively.

FIRST LABOURER Fifty odd boxes is correct,
               gov'nor, and main and mortal
               heavy they were too. Shiftin'
               that lot were thirsty work
               I can tell you.

SECOND LABOURER It were 'ard lines there
               wasn't no gentleman such,
               like yourself to show some
               sort of appreciation of
               our efforts in liquid form,
               Squire. We're so dry we can
               'ardly talk, still.

QUINCEY   Here, take a gargle - on the house.

He flicks a coin to the SECOND LABOURER who winks at
his mate.

SECOND LABOURER Thanks, Squire, that'll 'elp
                lay the dust.

FIRST LABOURER Blimey, it were that thick;
               you could 'ave slep' on it
               without 'urting yer bones.

SECOND LABOURER Not that you'd want to, mind!
                Me and me mate we thought we
                wouldn't never get out that
                old chapel quick enough.

FIRST LABOURER Took the cake it did Lor'!
               I wouldn't take less nor a
               quid to stay there after dark.
               I was that relieved when we
               turned the lock on it,
               I can't tell you.

QUINCEY   What about the key? Describe it.

SECOND VAMPIRE WOMAN It were a queer design on
                     a big rusty ring.

FIRST LABOURER We dropped it through the letter
               box of the big house as per
               Mr. Quennel's instructions.

He nods to the man in question who is hurrying out
of a nearby building towards them carrying a sheaf
of papers.

MR. QUENNEL No order form, no receipt,
            Mr. Morris. The cashier received
            payment for express delivery
            to Carfax in cash. The customer
            was new and unknown to her.
            A tall gentleman in black with -
            a foreign accent according
            to her recollection. He gave
            her the key and instructions

88

                    which I, in turn, passed on
                    to the men. We did right I
                    trust in shipping the consignment?

Quincey is still annoyed at his own negligence.

QUINCEY   Yeah, I gave him the go-ahead myself.

MR. QUENNEL Is there anything further
                    we can do for you?

QUINCEY   Just put me on the road to
                    Carfax and make sure it passes
                    a kiddie's toy store on the way.

The men look at Quincey in amazement.

EXT. CARFAX ESTATE. DAY.

QUINCEY walks up the steps of the shuttered house
and halts at the front door. From a coloured paper
bag he takes a child's periscope - a slim cardboard
affair housing an angled mirror at either end. Pushing it half-way through the horizontal letter box
he peers in to observe the floor inside the house,
adjusting the toy a little in the process.

INSERT: Dusty floorboards on which rests an
                    old key affixed to a rusty ring.

Quincey straightens up and takes a box out of the
bag containing a child's fishing rod. He assembles
it quickly and inserts it into the letter box and
with the aid of the periscope manages to hook the
ring, wind it up to the opening and extract it with
a little smile at his own ingenuity. Satisfied that
no one is watching, he puts his toys back in their
bag and sets off in search of:

THE CHAPEL: Surrounded by brambles and covered by
creeper, this Gothic edifice presents a daunting as-
pect to QUINCEY as he approaches it in the light of
the setting sun. The key fits, the lock turns. He
pushes the door open and enters.

INT. CHAPEL. DUSK.

A state of decay, if not absolute ruin is an ominous setting for the fifty boxes stacked in the form of an unusual pyramid. Saints in niches gaze stonily down at QUINCEY as he takes a crowbar from his bag and prepares to prize open the first casket until the sound of something approaching through the undergrowth sends him diving for cover. The dishevelled figure of RENFIELD enters carrying the limp, dead body of the GARDENER'S BOY which he offers up with tear-stained eyes to the topmost casket of the pile.

RENFIELD   Oh Master, even as Abraham
                was called by God to take his
                son Isaac into the wilderness
                as holy sacrifice, so I, your
                servant Renfield, offer up
                the body of this youth to the
                eternal glory of thy blessed
                name. Give me the kiss of peace
                that I may forever walk in
                your shadow and drink the blood
                of life everlasting ...

As Renfield drops his head in humility he notices something which gives him pause - wet footprints leading behind an adjacent tomb. Continuing his prayers so as to allay suspicion, Renfield gently lays the body down and poises himself for the attack.

RENFIELD   ... for as Saul slew in his
                thousands, David slew in his
                tens of thousands ...

With a spring like a wildcat he is over the top and tearing at Quincey, taken completely off his guard. Despite the fact that the Texan is as tough as nails he is no match for the madmen imbued with super-strength. After a short, fierce struggle, Quincey manages to slip from his grasp only to be caught, seconds later, in his flight up the crazy pyramid as the last rays of the dying sun slide down the topmost casket.

RENFIELD   And as the sun goes down on
the death of another day let
the sight of the Lord of Darkness
shine forth in all its majesty
bringing light to the sons and
daughters of darkness who forever
perpetuate his glory by draining
the unrighteous of all sin, and
converting them to life eternal
that they may sing his praise
forever, and ever, amen, amen ...

Renfield continually repeats himself as he forces the struggling Quincey towards the topmost casket, the lid of which is slowing beginning to rise, emitting a fantastical light of supernatural power. Simultaneously there is an enormous inrush of air which causes the stained glass in all the windows to crack and disintegrate, the organ pipes to scream and centuries of dust to spin in a glittering whirlwind. Gradually, Renfield forces Quincey closer and closer to the blinding light of the casket until he sees inside DRACULA, whose skeleton is pulsating through his clothed body like an atomic x-ray.
Now the heart is seen beating and the blood racing through his veins. Now his eyes flicker open, now his lips are bared, revealing the pointed teeth, now a smile of anticipation as he starts to rise up towards the bared flesh of Quincey's throat held in the lunatic's grip of iron. The cacophony reaches a crescendo just as Dracula's teeth are about to make contact with his latest victim.
Then Renfield is being pulled back by FOUR ORDERLIES as Doberman Pinchers tear at his limbs and DR. SEWARD and VAN HELSING wrestle Quincey from his grasp. Thwarted, Dracula's smile turns to a sneer of hatred and then to one of triumph as Quincey empties a colt revolver harmlessly into his levitating body. A moment later, Dracula is drawn into the whirling incandescent dust until, with a mighty beating of oily black wings, he flies forth through the shattered, gaping windows into the darkening night, like a creature from Dante's Inferno. All faces watch his triumphant flight in complete awe.

INT. SANATORIUM. DR. SEWARD'S DRAWING ROOM. NIGHT.

While VAN HELSING studies a pile of tomes from London, DR. SEWARD paces restlessly up and down under a heavy burden of guilt. QUINCEY is slumped in a chair near the fire sipping a brandy, his hatred for Dracula bowing only to his grief for Lucy.

DR. SEWARD   ... of course I am responsible,
              if Renfield had been adequately
              supervised ...

VAN HELSING (interrupting) Those iron bars were
              adequate enough for ten madmen!

DR. SEWARD   I have two deaths on my hands,
              Professor.

VAN HELSING They were victims of occult powers,
              not medical negligence.
              Don't reproach yourself.

But Quincey is reluctant to believe that Lucy was associated with the creature in the chapel in any way.

QUINCEY   How can you be certain Lucy
              didn't die from natural causes?
              We all know she was a sick lady ...

VAN HELSING Because the wound on her
              throat was deeper than before,
              and the skin more bruised.

DR. SEWARD   And despite the transfusion,
              her death was caused by a
              massive loss of blood.

VAN HELSING Of which there is no sign.

Still, Quincey is reluctant to accept the idea.

QUINCEY   And nobody saw anything
              strange at all?

DR. SEWARD   Except for a brief period
              when there were no visitors

                    or callers, Nurse Danvers
                    was with her the whole time.

VAN HELSING   My theory is Renfield
                    admitted him.

DR. SEWARD   He says not.

Van Helsing brushes his objection aside.

VAN HELSING   All the signs point to it.

DR. SEWARD   But Renfield didn't break
                    out until this afternoon.

VAN HELSING   The cell has a window -
                    our vampire can adopt any shape
                    or substance he desires;
                    he is the highest form of
                    Nosferatu ...

Both men look at him quizzically.

VAN HELSING   The Undead. Cursed with -
                    immortality they cannot die
                    but must go on from age to
                    age seeking new victims;
                    for all that die from the bite
                    of the Undead become themselves
                    Undead and must drink of human
                    blood forever.

DR. SEWARD   (interrupting) What we saw was a mass
                    hallucination. Vampires are
                    creatures of folk lore
                    and superstition.

VAN HELSING   (exploding) Superstition is the name
                    we scientists give to matters
                    beyond the limitations of our
                    factual minds. Unless you can
                    prove it by science you do not
                    accept the proof of your own
                    eyes. What greater scientific
                    argument for death than six
                    bullets fired into a human body?

                              93

Poof! When science fails we must
turn to superstition or, as I
prefer to call it, tradition.
And tradition knew vampires in
old Greece, ancient Rome, also
the Balkans where the peoples
fear him to this day. They know
the vampire lives on, and cannot
die by mere passage of time.

Fired by the Professor's rhetoric, Quincey adopts a
more positive attitude.

QUINCEY   Okay, Professor, so how do we kill
                 this vampire - by tradition?

Van Helsing is delighted he has a convert.

VAN HELSING Tradition says that if your bullet
                 had been sacred he would be dead
                 evermore. A wooden stake hammered
                 through the heart and the severing
                 of the head will also turn the
                 Undead into true dead.

QUINCEY   So what's our first move, Professor?

VAN HELSING We must first sterilize the
                 poisoned earth in each of his
                 boxes wherein he can rest in
                 safety in the hours of daylight.
                 Then he can have no refuge
                 from dawn to sunset when he
                 is most weak, for like all
                 evil things, his power ceases
                 at the coming of day. Only his
                 earth can save him.

QUINCEY   But why does he need so much,
                 Professor? There's enough dirt
                 there for a whole swarm of vampires.

VAN HELSING His empire he plans to spread
                 wide. Soon to every corner of
                 the realm he will despatch his
                 caskets of earth so he may rest

                    in safety in the day and prey
                    on his victims at night until
                    the Undead will run amok
                    throughout the kingdom.

QUINCEY   When we exterminate rats we
                    burn the critters out.

VAN HELSING   To purge evil with fire is
                    not enough. With prayers and
                    holy water it must also be
                    driven out of the very ashes
                    hissing like a dying serpent.

DR. SEWARD who has been listening with scepticism
begins to catch the enthusiasm of the others.

DR. SEWARD   We've paraffin in plenty and
                    there's holy water in the chapel.

VAN HELSING   Our plan must be accomplished
                    before sunrise; now make a go of it!

QUINCEY (quietly) Before we start, I'd like
                    to pay my last respects to Lucy.

Lucy's death has done nothing to draw the ex-rivals
closer together and it is only after a moment's
hesitation that Dr. Seward nods in acquiescence and
leads the way from the room.

INT. MORGUE. NIGHT.

White tiles, caged lights and marble slabs on one of
which lies the GARDENER'S BOY. LUCY is stretched out
on another surrounded by THREE MEN - lost in their
private thoughts until the ringing of a telephone
calls Dr. Seward to a darkened corner.

DR. SEWARD (brusquely) Hello, Seward speaking.

MINA'S VOICE Hello, Doctor, this is Mina Murray.

DR. SEWARD (frowning) Oh, hello, er look,
                    I'm terribly pressed for time,
                    can I call you back tomorrow?

MINA'S VOICE (desperately) Oh, Doctor, please!
I must see you! It's urgent!
My fiancé Jonathan Harker has some
important information for you.
It might prove vital in your
treatment of Lucy.

DR. SEWARD wants the conversation, which is becoming
increasingly awkward, over and done with.

DR. SEWARD   Look, I have to leave now on
an urgent call. I may not be
back until dawn.

MINA'S VOICE (urgently) Then we'll wait up
for you, please.

Seeing the battle is lost, Dr. Seward submits gracefully.

DR. SEWARD   Of course! I shall have a
room set aside for you. And
now if you have a pencil I
will give you directions.

As he prepares to do so we return to the TWO MEN
contemplating the beautiful corpse.

QUINCEY   She looks so innocent
Professor, so pure.

VAN HELSING And by the grace of God
she will remain so ...

He reverently touches the crucifix hanging round Lucy's
neck.

VAN HELSING ... so long as this crucifix hangs
about her neck she will never be
Nosferatu. And she will be buried
thus in a sealed coffin.

QUINCEY (doubtfully) That little trinket is enough
to keep her soul at peace?

VAN HELSIN (nodding) It places her beyond
the reach of all evil.

QUINCEY   Even from our friend?

VAN HELSING   He may not enter anywhere
               unless someone of the household
               bids him come.

QUINCEY   How about Renfield, couldn't
               he do the inviting?

VAN HELSING   Renfield is in a padded
               cell deep in the cellars.
               In a strait-jacket.

The sound of the bell as Dr. Seward rings off acts
as a signal for the night's work to begin. Quincey
tenderly kisses the dead sweetheart on the forehead
then hurries after his friends. The light is extin-
guished, the doorcloses.

EXT. CHAPEL. NIGHT.

The old stone walls glitter red, the empty windows
seem to stare in wonder at the bonfire of boxes blazing
 forth in a small clearing nearby. FOUR ORDERLIES
are consigning the last of the caskets to the flames
while VAN HELSING, DR. SEWARD, and QUINCEY watch
with troubled faces.

DR. SEWARD   Forty-nine it is, Quincey,
               no matter how you count them.

QUINCEY   I ain't arguin', Doc.
               I counted 'em myself three
               times, but I just can't figure
               it out. Down at the dock they
               told me the full consignment
               was delivered right here.

VAN HELSING   In the morning, first thing,
               we must trace it. So long as
               one box remains he has refuge
               and we are endangered.

At this moment, an Orderly approaches from the direction of the hospital for a word with Dr. Seward.

```
ORDERLY        Dr. Seward, the lady and gentleman
               have arrived. She wanted to see you
               at once but I explained that was
               not possible.

DR. SEWARD     Did you show them to their quarters?

ORDERLY        Yes, sir. The gentleman with a
               broken arm turned in straight away.
               He seemed rather poorly. The lady
               is waiting up and has asked to see
               you directly you get back.
```

EXT. SANITORIUM GUEST ROOM. NIGHT.

MINA is staring with curiosity at the distant blaze
which is reflected in the window giving the momentary
impression that she is on fire. Behind her, in the
darkened room, a dim shape materializes as a figure
in white soundlessly approaches and finally taps Mina
on the shoulder causing her to spin round in surprise.
It is LUCY.

INT. SANATORIUM GUEST ROOM. NIGHT.

LUCY smiles sweetly as if meeting her friend in these
circumstances was the most natural thing in the
world. MINA, after her initial shock, is pleased to
see her though obviously concerned for her well-be-
ing and takes her warmly by the hand.

```
MINA           Oh Lucy, thank God you're safe.
               When there was no reply from the
               house I guessed you'd be here.
               But I must say I thought you'd
               be in bed at this hour.

LUCY           How nice to see you, Mina.
               Are you alone?

MINA (whispering) No, Jonathan's with me; he's
               in there, asleep. I'm waiting
               to see Dr. Seward about him -
               he's far from well.
```

Through an open door we see JONATHAN HARKER, with his arm in a sling, asleep on the bed in the next room.

LUCY   Poor Jonathan, what has he done
                    to himself?

Mina quietly closes the door and turns back to her friend.

MINA (shivering) Broken an arm for one thing.
                    It's cold in here; let me get you
                    my wrap.

Lucy allows herself to be led towards the glowing fire where Mina leaves her in order to get her wrap from the closet. Then, as Lucy stands before the flames, Mina drapes the garment around her shoulders and with all the force at her command hurls Lucy into the open closet and, before she can recover has bolted the door. Falling against it she lets go of the control she mastered so adroitly and gives way to emotion.

LUCY'S VOICE Mina, what on earth are you doing?
                    Open the door at once.
                    Is this a game? If anything
                    should happen to me you'll be
                    personally responsible to
                    Dr. Seward, do you hear?

With an effort, Mina forces herself away from the voice of her old friend and runs from the room for help.

INT. SANATORIUM CORRIDOR. NIGHT.

Muffled shouts and murmurs greet MINA as she runs hopefully towards the figure of a retreating ORDERLY.

MINA (shouting) Please, you must help me.
                    as Dr. Seward returned yet?

Slowly the Orderly turns round. Unknown to Mina he is nevertheless familiar to us. It is RENFIELD.

RENFIELD   Dr. Seward returned yet?

Renfield shakes his head and looks at her strangely.

MINA   Please, I must speak to someone in
               authority. His deputy, the duty officer;
               surely there must be someone in charge?

RENFIELD   In charge?

Renfield smiles, nods and turning on his heel crosses
the hall, opens a door and beckons Mina to follow
him into -

INT. LECTURE ROOM. NIGHT.

Darkness except for a large illuminated heart projected
onto a screen. The shuffle of vague figures and a dis-
embodied voice intoning a lecture are the immediate
impressions which hit MINA as she stumbles blindly
through the door. The dominating voice, new to her,
is no stranger to us. It is:

THE VOICE OF DRACULA Human blood is made up of
               plasma and red cells.
               For every 3.8 fluid ounces of blood,
               there are two fluid ounces of plasma,
               and 1.8 fluid ounces of red cells.
               Plasma makes up 4.3 percent of the total
               body weight, and normally red cells account
               for 4.2 percent.
               Therefore, 8.5 percent of the body's weight
               is blood. The human body has a blood volume
               of about 12 pints.
               Blood flows through the body at a rate of
               1.6 to 3.3 feet per second and increases
               steadily as it nears the heart.
               2.4 pints of blood flow through the kidneys
               per minute. 1.5 pints of blood flow through
               the brain per minute. 2.5 pints of blood
               flow through the liver per minute.
               The heart's estimated weight is 11 ounces.
               The heart's volume is about 20 fluid ounces.
               The heart's blood volume is eight fluid
               ounces. It takes 8/10th of a second
               for the heart to contract.

The heart of a normal resting adult ejects a
volume of 2.6 fluid ounces for every stroke.
The heart beats 72 times per minute.
The heart puts out a blood volume of 10 pints
per minutes. In heavy exercise the cardiac
output is 40 to 50 pints per minute,
using five-and-a-half pints of oxygen
per minute at a corresponding rate of
180 strokes per minute, and an increase
of 50 percent in its stroke volume.

By now, Mina is beside herself with impatience and
turns once more to Renfield dimly visible at her side
by the light of the changing slides illustrating the
lecture.

MINA   Look, it's imperative I talk to
            somebody at once.
            It's really most urgent.

RENFIELD   You had best speak to the Master;
            he will not keep you long.

Mina does her best to curb her anxiety while the
discourse on blood takes a more poetic turn and continues with illustrations of increasing excitement
and imagination.

THE VOICE OF DRACULA Blood is the colour of precious
            stones. Of rubies, garnets.
            Blood is the colour of fire, of lava, of power,
            of planets. Blood is the colour of courage,
            of magic. Blood is the colour of the setting
            sun. Blood is the colour of life in darkness.
            Life beyond the grave. Life eternal.
            The Blood is the Life.

The unseen patients chant the message repeatedly.

VOICES   The Blood is the Life ...
            The Blood is the Life ...

The chant becomes a hypnotic pulse, almost like the
beating of a giant heart. And on the screen the images
have become a pulsating psychedelic vision, a vision
which Mina finds herself compulsively drawn toward.

Closer and closer she approaches the vision until it surrounds and envelops her. DRACULA'S head possesses her, her clothes melt from her body. The heartbeat controls her, and grips her body in compulsive spasms which she seems unable and unwilling to subdue. She rides the bucking red waves wantonly with growing frenzy. Gradually Dracula's hands travel up her body and cover her breasts followed by her head which rises up to cover her face as they engage in a passionate kiss. The CAMERA zooms into their lips.

The chanting metamorphoses into a wild grunting, panting throb! At climax, the mouth of the lovers part and Mina's gushes blood as she screams in ecstasy.

BLACK OUT:

EXT. CARFAX ESTATE. NIGHT.

A gagged figure, seemingly armless, stumbles wide-eyed through trees and brambles towards the blackened pile which is all that remains of the caskets of Dracula. VAN HELSING, DR. SEWARD, and QUINCEY pause in their work of sprinkling the steaming ashes with holy water to take in the bizarre sight. As the figure approaches we see it is constrained by a strait-jacket.

VAN HELSING Renfield has escaped.

Quincey dives for his feet and brings him down.

DR. SEWARD   STOP! It's one of the orderlies!

Bending over him, Doctor Seward removes the gag from his mouth, and is amazed when it is followed by a golden crucifix on a chain.

VAN HELSING My crucifix, my God!

QUINCEY   He's stolen it from Lucy
             - you dirty ghoul!

The thief who was almost on his feet is knocked down again by one of Quincey's flying fists. Dr. Seward restrains him.

DR. SEWARD   I told you. It's Marlow,
                  he's an orderly. Help me
                  release him.

Quincey reluctantly complies.

QUINCEY   Okay Mister, explain how you
                  got a'hold of that trinket.

VAN HELSING   He has robbed the dead and
                  has suffered the consequences.
                  Soon we shall suffer them
                  also.

DR. SEWARD   Speak up, Marlow, are you guilty?

The freed man nods, speaking between gasps.

MARLOW   I stole yes; what use is gold
                  to the dead? Before I got to
                  the door I felt her hand on my
                  shoulder, like ice.
                  (he shudders at the macabre memory)

MARLOW   She spun me round. I saw her face -
                  evil it was, and her teeth were
                  sharp, and then she threw me
                  against the slab. Such strength!
                  My head hit the marble. When I
                  came to I was like this. I saw
                  no one. I remembered the flames,
                  the door was open, I escaped ...

The three men have been listening with growing
concern and all talk at once.

DR. SEWARD   How about the rest of the staff?

MARLOW   I saw no one.

VAN HELSING   Dracula is now master of the
                  sanatorium, and this is his
                  message of defiance.

DR. SEWARD   Miss Murray, and Harker -
                  was there no sign of my guests?

Marlow shakes his head.

DR. SEWARD ... nothing, you saw nothing?
Was there no sound? Did you hear
nothing?

MARLOW (reluctantly) I heard voice chanting:
"The blood is the life" ...

INT. SANATORIUM GUEST BEDROOM. NIGHT.

Words now give way to music as the images of this
night of horror orchestrate themselves into a visual
symphony of the macabre. LUCY raises her head. Her
mouth drips blood in the moonlight. She looks like
a wild animal disturbed while engorging its prey.
Suddenly a dazzling light in the form of a cross
hits her face. Screaming, she drags her naked body
away from that of her victim, JONATHAN HARKER, and
sliding from the bed retreats into a corner.

And all the time the glowing cross follows her as VAN
HELSING with a torch masked to give this cruciform
effect advances on her accompanied by QUINCEY and
DR. SEWARD carrying a strait-jacket of black leather
and chains. Her strength drains by the power of the
holy light. Lucy is finally trapped, restrained and
manacled. As the Professor places his golden crucifix
once more around her neck, Lucy's screams and strug-
gles cease altogether.

DISSOLVE TO: INT. SANATORIUM CELLAR. NIGHT.

QUINCEY and VAN HELSING unlock the door of a padded
cell to find TWELVE members of the STAFF gagged and
trussed in strait-jackets. They set about releasing
them.

DISSOLVE TO: INT. LECTURE ROOM. NIGHT.

DR. SEWARD carries the unconscious MINA draped in
a white sheet up the steps of the deserted room
towards the exit.

DISSOLVE TO:

INT. OPERATING THEATRE. NIGHT.

LUCY is strapped down to the operating table. QUINCEY, eyes closed and trembling with emotion holds a sharp wooden stake against the tight leather of the strait-jacket directly above her heart. Lucy's eyes stare wide with horror as she spits at VAN HELSING who brings down a heavy mallet onto the stake with all his might. Lucy screams as blood spurts from the wound.

INT. PRIVATE WARD. NIGHT.

TWO ORDERLIES lift JONATHAN HARKER from a stretcher and into a bed next to the sleeping MINA who is also still unconscious. DR. SEWARD turns from attending to her blood transfusion to do the same for Jonathan.

INT. OPERATING THEATRE. NIGHT.

VAN HELSING finishes severing Lucy's head from her body and places it on the operating table between her outstretched legs. QUINCEY turns his eyes away in horror. We see that the stake is embedded deep in her heart. Lucy's body quivers into stillness. As the Professor closes her eyes, the music, which has run as a graphic counterpoint, ends on a note of repose.

DISSOLVE TO: THE SEA and the restful sound of the sea. A lone ship steams toward the horizon followed by a solitary SWIMMER whose strokes become progressively weaker until with a pitiful cry of 'Master!', RENFIELD sinks beneath the waves.

MINA (voice-over) I hear the sound of rushing
                water ... and a throbbing ...
            as that of a great heart.

DISSOLVE TO: MINA'S FACE, eyes closed, in:

INT. THE PRIVATE WARD. DAY.

VAN HELSING is at her bedside, questioning her.

VAN HELSING What do you see?

MINA   I see nothing. It is dark.

JONATHAN HARKER in the next bed, pale through loss
of blood, is more concerned with Mina's condition
than his own.

JONATHAN   We were both attacked,
              Professor. We both suffered
              a great loss of blood; why
              is she still unconscious?

VAN HELSING   Lucy took your blood. She is
              twice dead and has no claim on you.
              The blood of Miss Mina flows in
              the veins of another, and her
              blood speaks. If she is the
              victim of your Count Dracula
              as I suspect, then the seeds of
              his own destruction he has sown.

JONATHAN   You mean she could lead us to him?

VAN HELSING   Over the water ...

JONATHAN   ... to Castle Dracula?

VAN HELSING   If my theory is correct.

As Mina's eyes begin to flicker open, there is a
brief knock and QUINCEY pokes his head around the
door.

QUINCEY   Can you spare a minute, Professor?

VAN HELSING nods, gets up and has a final word with
Jonathan.

VAN HELSING   I leave you together. Your turn
              it is now to be physician;
              gently, gently. Later we will talk.

As the Professor closes the door, Jonathan gets out
of bed and takes Mina in his arms so that when she
regains total consciousness, she will be comforted.

INT. SANATORIUM CORRIDOR. DAY.

The Professor takes QUINCEY by the arm and walks him
away from the steady STREAM OF PATIENTS being escorted by members of the STAFF back into their rooms.

VAN HELSING   Well, what news you have for me?
               Good, bad, you found it, yes?

QUINCEY   I tracked down the box, sure.
               It was damaged in the unloading.
               They were going to fix it and
               sent it on to Carfax today.

VAN HELSING   (urgently) You apprehended it?

QUINCEY   Too late. The order was
               countermanded. It was shipped
               off at dawn today on the boat train...

VAN HELSING   That would be the Magyar Express.
               My theory is working out.

But Quincey is too full of his own theories to ask
about the Professor's.

QUINCEY   ... so we've got him, Professor.
               All we have to do is fly to
               France and ambush the train
               before the box is unloaded.

And the Professor has little time for Quincey's theory
either.

VAN HELSING   I doubt we could make Calais in time.
               Our best chance would be Vienna.

QUINCEY (truculent) Vienna! How do you know
               he's headed that far?

VAN HELSING   (positively) Because he's going home!
               All the signs point to it throughout
               history, from his defeat in Turkey
               centuries ago right up to the present
               time. Whenever he was in danger he fled
               back over the sea to Castle Dracula.

QUINCEY   Castle Dracula; what in
                 tarnation's that?

VAN HELSING Dracula's objective, Quincey,
                 and yours ...

He catches sight of DR. SEWARD and a group of his
staff and patients at the far end of the corridor and
starts back towards him followed by Quincey.

VAN HELSING ... Should we miss him on the
                 train you and Dr. Seward will
                 be waiting for him there. You
                 will make a well-balanced team.

Quincey is not so sure.

VAN HELSING ... We will need maps of the
                 Carpathians, arms and ammunition;
                 for two parties - we must divide
                 forces. Go like the wind and
                 return like the whirlwind.

QUINCEY   Your darn tootin' Professor.

The promise of high adventure quells any reserva-
tions Quincey has concerning Dr. Seward as a partner
and he runs off to prepare for the journey. Meanwhile, Dr. Seward has finished his conversation with
STAFF and PATIENTS, who begin to disperse, and turns
to the Professor.

DR. SEWARD   Any progress, Professor?

VAN HELSING Yes, but we must move fast.
                 Are your patients all tucked up
                 in bed with their Ovaltine?

DR. SEWARD   (nodding) No harm done; they were all
                 wandering about the grounds
                 in a hypnotic trance.
                 With the exception of Renfield;
                 he's still missing.

VAN HELSING   Poor Renfield. If Miss Mina's
              attacker was this Count Dracula
              of Jonathan's then Renfield's
              miracle cure in Transylvania and
              his involvement with our vampire
              all tie up ...

They re-enter: THE PRIVATE WARD:

MINA is fully awake, although very pale, sitting up
in bed with JONATHAN at her side holding her hand,
which he relinquishes to DR. SEWARD who takes her
pulse. Urgency causes VAN HELSING to dispense with
ceremony.

VAN HELSING   Well, are they one and the same,
              our vampire, and your Count Dracula?

JONATHAN   According to Mina's description,
              'yes', without a doubt. Mina,
              this is Professor Van Helsing.

VAN HELSING   Miss Murray, you have just
              undergone a tremendous ordeal,
              not only on your own account
              but also with the loss of poor
              Lucy, and in ...

MINA (interrupting) Her hands were icy,
              and her teeth -
              (she shudders)
              I knew ...
              (pulling herself together)
              I understand from Jonathan
              that you feel I might be in
              some kind of supernatural
              contact with my attacker.

VAN HELSING   You started talking in your sleep;
              I asked you questions, you responded.
              I made a simple deduction.

MINA   You wish us to join you in
              tracking him down?

Dr. Seward frowns, considering Mina unfit for such an expedition.

VAN HELSING   If you are strong enough, yes.
               By hypnotising you we may learn
               things of which your conscious
               self is unaware.

The strain is beginning to tell on Dr. Seward who wishes the whole thing over and done with.

DR. SEWARD   She's not fit to travel. Why
               can't we all forget about it?

The Professor looks at him gravely for a moment before replying.

VAN HELSING   Because this dog can live for
               centuries and she is but a mortal
               woman. Time is to be dreaded -
               now that he has put that mark
               upon her throat.

Dr. Seward pulls himself together while Mina gives way to a moment of despair.

MINA   Oh, God, you should have let me die.

Jonathan puts his arm around her shoulder comfortingly.

VAN HELSING   (sternly) Until Dracula is dead
               you must not die or you will become
               ever as himself, the living Un-Dead.
               You must live! You must struggle
               and strive to live, to fight
               death himself though he come
               to you in pain or in joy; by
               the day or the night; in safety
               or in peril. On your living soul
               I charge that you do not die -
               not even think of death - till
               this evil will be past.

Van Helsing's energy transmits itself to Mina who takes on new strength.

MINA   Very well, I promise!

The Professor takes from his pocket the crucifix
which once adorned Lucy.

VAN HELSING And fear not, we shall protect
             you from evil at all times.

So saying he places the crucifix around her neck with
a startling consequence - sizzling flesh, as the
cross touches her bare skin! Quickly, the Professor
rips it from her as Mina screams in agony.

INT. CAB. VIENNA. DAY.

As the vehicle races through the streets, JONATHAN
and VAN HELSING face MINA who is under hypnosis.

VAN HELSING Try harder! Shut out all noise
             of the motor. Listen not with
             your ears, but with the blood
             flowing in the veins of Dracula.
             His heart pumps your blood.
             What does it hear?

Mina groans and seems to speak from another plane.

MINA   Footsteps, voices, the hissing
             of snakes!

JONATHAN   That must be steam.

The Professor motions him to be silent.

VAN HELSING And what does your blood - feel?

MINA   It's floating, now lurching,
             now a shock, a bump, and now
             stillness.

VAN HELSING And what does it see, your blood?

MINA   It sees ...

She appears to be having a desperate mental struggle.

MINA   It means a ...
              (suddenly the struggle is over)
              ... darkness, like the grave.

Exhausted, her head falls to one side. Jonathan is
disturbed.

JONATHAN   That's enough, Professor.
              I don't like it. It's obvious
              Dracula's in his casket on
              board the train. The movement,
              the bump, it's as clear as day.

The Professor overcomes his own misgivings with a
grunt and endeavours to bring Mina out of her trance.

VAN HELSING   Return, Miss Mina. Listen to
              the beat of your own heart.
              Return ... Return ...

Jonathan glances anxiously at his wrist-watch.

JONATHAN   Only three minutes, Professor,
              we'll never do it.

Mina opens her eyes with a blink and smiles.

INT. VIENNA. THE WEST BAHNHOF STATION. DAY.

VAN HELSING, MINA and JONATHAN race down the platform towards CAMERA until a trellised metal gate
shoots across cutting off any further progress though
their momentum carries them into it with a crash of
frustration.

CUT TO: THEIR POINT OF VIEW:

Through the trellis we see the PORTER responsible
for closing the gate blow his whistle. The engine of
the Magyar Express toots in return.

CUT TO: The disappointed faces of the travellers.

CUT TO: The DRIVER of the train releasing the brake.
Suddenly a safety valve blows causing both him and
the FIREMAN to adopt various safety measures.

CUT TO: The PORTER listening to their shouts until another shout causes him to look at the travellers on the other side of the gate, one of whom is brandishing a golden coin.

VAN HELSING (in German) Please my good man,
              the train is delayed. Accept
              this and let us on board.
              It is a matter of life and death.

Seeing another ENGINEER climb onto the footplate with a big spanner, the Porter quickly grabs the coin, slides open the gate and directs the trio along the platform to a carriage door which he unlocks.

INSERT: SPANNER tightening a nut on the safety valve. Whistle blowing. Driver waving. Wheels turning.

<u>INT. FIRST CLASS COMPARTMENT. DAY.</u>

The THREE TRAVELLERS, hardly able to credit their good fortune, catch their breath and as the station slips away begin to make plans.

VAN HELSING   How far, Jonathan, from Vienna
              to Budapest is it?

JONATHAN   No more than 150 miles, Professor.
              We're due there in 98 minutes.

VAN HELSING   Go, Jonathan! See if our little
              clairvoyant's prophecy was correct
              - there is not time to waste.

JONATHAN   Right ho, Professor.

He slips quickly out of the compartment and makes off down the corridor.

MINA   And is Vienna the closest spot
              to Castle Dracula?

VAN HELSING   Our route, in truth, goes
              considerably nearer, but
              Budapest is the first stop
              and I speculate the casket

                    there will be unloaded,
                    by which time he will be
                    true dead and you will be
                    free to marry your Jonathan.

He kisses her hand gallantly at which Mina laughs a
little strangely, but before the Professor has time
to consider why, Jonathan returns with the news.

JONATHAN   Just as we guessed. The box is
                there, there's no mistaking it -
                also a guard, worst luck, who
                looks like part of the furniture.

VAN HELSING He would an embarrassing spectator be.

JONATHAN   And an even worse witness.

VAN HELSING Perhaps soon he will the tickets check.

JONATHAN   And what if he doesn't? Before
                you know it we'll be in Budapest.

MINA (brightly) Why the long faces? It couldn't
                be simpler; all we have to do is
                pull the communication cord and
                stop the train. The guard will
                leave his van to investigate
                and you will be waiting outside
                ready to go in and do your work.

VAN HELSING How strongly the casket is
                sealed we know not.

JONATHAN   It may be a long job and when
                the guard sees nothing is up
                he'll come straight back.

MINA   Not before he has retrieved my hat ...

Both men look at her in puzzlement.

MINA   When he asks me why I pulled
                the cord I'll say that my hat,
                with the diamond brooch, blew
                out of the window.

JONATHAN   I hope he doesn't realise it's paste.

VAN HELSING   As long as her tears are real
               he will be convinced.

MINA   Nothing false about them, I promise.

JONATHAN   It's a good idea.

VAN HELSING   We must a move on get.

He lifts his old Gladstone bag from the rack.

VAN HELSING   Two minutes, Miss Mina, then pull!

JONATHAN   Sit tight, my love, in a little
               while you'll be free of him forever.

He kisses her on the mouth and follows the Professor through the door into the corridor. Mina watches
them go with a distant smile which just reveals the
points of her newly sharp teeth.

INT. TRAIN CORRIDOR. DAY.

VAN HELSING and JONATHAN duck into a Third Class
compartment next to the Guard's van and wait.

INT. FIRST CLASS COMPARTMENT. DAY.

MINA counts the passing seconds to herself then pulls
the wire. With a squeal of brakes that nearly sends
her flying, the train begins to rapidly decelerate.

INT. THIRD CLASS COMPARTMENT. DAY.

VAN HELSING and JONATHAN see the GUARD rush by the
window along the corridor, then with a glance at each
other, run out of the door in the opposite direction.

INT. FIRST CLASS COMPARTMENT. DAY.

MINA, now hatless, is found in heated conversation
with the GUARD just as the train enters a tunnel
and begins to slip into darkness. MINA and the Guard
talk simultaneously:

MINA   ... on the hat band was an
                    extremely valuable diamond
                    brooch. You can see for yourself
                    what happened. In lowering the
                    window it was whisked off by
                    the wind and ...

GUARD (in German) I cannot understand what you
                    are saying; kindly speak German.
                    If you are trying to tell me
                    you stopped the train because your
                    hat blew out of the window, then
                    you will be prosecuted Madam, and ...

During the conversation, the carriage lights come on
and the train grinds to a standstill.

INT. GUARD'S VAN. DAY.

VAN HELSING and JONATHAN are feverishly working on
the lid of Dracula's casket with crow-bars. The wood
is beginning to splinter.

INT. FIRST CLASS COMPARTMENT. DAY.

MINA and the GUARD are still at loggerheads.

MINA   I insist you organize a search
                    immediately. That brooch is worth
                    a small fortune ...

GUARD (interrupting in German) Madame,
                    the train has been delayed long
                    enough. Losing your hat does not
                    constitute an emergency.

The GUARD who is looking out of the window sees
something which causes him to blink in disbelief.

GUARD'S POINT OF VIEW:

Silhouettes of HORSEMEN seen against the mouth of
the tunnel in the distance are galloping towards
CAMERA. They are escorting a cart.

RESUME:

FIRST CLASS COMPARTMENT

The GUARD runs out of the door with a cry of outrage.

EXT. TRAIN.

The GUARD jumps down and runs towards the HORSEMEN who have now reached the Guard's van.

INT. GUARD'S VAN. DAY.

VAN HELSING and JONATHAN with a mighty effort throw back the lid. The casket is empty. Their alarm is deepened by the sound of shots literally outside the main doors.

EXT. GUARD'S VAN. DAY.

GYPSY BANDITS shoot the GUARD full of holes as he attempts to stop them breaking open the door.

INT. GUARD'S VAN. DAY.

VAN HELSING and JONATHAN look at each other in dismay.

VAN HELSING   Dracula us has tricked!

JONATHAN   Mina, she's alone!

They run for the door leading to the corridor. To their surprise it is locked and despite their efforts refuses to budge. Retrieving their crow-bars they now apply them to the locked door. Meanwhile the main doors are beginning to splinter. Suddenly the lights go out.

INT. FIRST CLASS COMPARTMENT. DAY.

MINA stands in the semi-darkness illuminated by the faint light from the tunnel entrance filtering in through the window. A noise in the doorway sends her spinning round to face it. But it is too dark to see until a train passing in the other direction floods the carriage in a flickering light revealing - DRACULA.

117

DRACULA   Thank you, Mina, my sweet.

Mina smiles at her Master tenderly.

INT. GUARD'S VAN. DAY.

The doors are torn off by the BANDITS and the interior
hit by the strobing light of the roaring Express.
VAN HELSING and JONATHAN are shot at just as they
crash through the door into the corridor. The bandits
start pulling the casket out of the van.

INT. FIRST CLASS COMPARTMENT. DAY.

The flickering light illuminates MINA and DRACULA
embracing.

INT. TRAIN CORRIDOR. DAY.

JONATHAN scrambles to safety but stops when he sees
the shot VAN HELSING stumble and fall. He runs to
him and kneels at his side as the Express passes
leaving them in darkness with the sound of the departing bandits echoing down the tracks.

VAN HELSING   I'm all right; go to Mina - hurry!

JONATHAN   But Professor, you're not all right.

VAN HELSING   Hurry, I feel she is in danger.

JONATHAN   Come, you can't stay here.

He drags him the short distance along the corridor to:

INT. FIRST CLASS COMPARTMENT. DAY.

The lights come on as JONATHAN hauls VAN HELSING
through the doorway and lays him down on a seat.
Of Mina there is no sign. Everywhere is the sound
of confusion, frightened voices, PASSENGERS running
along the corridor, and shouting from outside. Jonathan
is distraught, but does his best for the Professor who
is coughing blood.

JONATHAN   She's gone. My God, Professor,
               I must try and find a doctor.

VAN HELSING   Leave me, I am finished.
               Go after them; every moment counts.
               You can do nothing for me. She is
               completely in his power. Everything
               she says comes through Dracula.
               Quickly, once the train
               starts you will never catch
               him. There will be questions,
               statements, police. GO!

Jonathan kisses the Professor on the forehead.

JONATHAN   God bless you, Professor.

Tearing himself away, he takes a Winchester and a
map from his bag and runs out of the door just as
the train starts moving.

EXT. TRAIN. DAY.

Jonathan jumps off as the train gathers momentum and is
left as a lone figure running along the track towards
the south of the tunnel.

EXT. WOODED ISLAND. NIGHT.

The BANDITS sit around a camp fire, eating and relax-
ing. A short distance away from the encampment on a
beach overlooking the sunlit waters of the swiftly
flowing river stands DRACULA with his arm around MINA.
He looks more romantic than ever. Mina is now more
beautiful than we have ever known her. Though she
is not one of the great artists he has dedicated his
life to save, Mina has an attraction Dracula finds
irresistible. He words his seduction accordingly.

DRACULA   You will share the delights
               of the earth with me forever.

MINA   To be 'Nosferatu' means to
               be exiled from God's love.

119

DRACULA   What is the love of God?
               Little by little he reveals
               to you the wonders of the earth,
               like a parent offering a child
               a glittering box of sweets, then
               just as you reach out eagerly,
               he snatches them away.
               Those whom he loves, die as
               quickly as May flies while we,
               whom he hates, live on and on.
               We enjoy everything, and give up
               nothing. No perfume the world has
               ever known escapes my memory.
               There is not a springtime of
               blossoms in 500 years that
               has not given me pleasure,
               barely a note of all the music
               ever written to which I have
               not danced. How jealously
               God guards his immortality.
               Shakespeare, Michelangelo,
               Tchaikovsky: as soon as they
               challenged him with their
               vision of heaven he cut them
               down - until we started to
               fight him.
               Now some of our greatest artists
               are 'Nosferatu'. But if it were
               known they would be persecuted
               for sorcery, demonology, persecuted
               for creating eternal beauty.
               So once in a lifetime they change
               their identity, even their style.

Mina finds the idea fantastic but is intrigued nevertheless.

MINA   Is that what drew you to Lucy?

DRACULA   Poor, sweet Lucy, whose
               golden voice would still be
               thrilling us today had she
               not been cut down in God's
               name by your friends.

MINA   It's incredible!

DRACULA   When one is immortal, one
                 cannot live by blood alone.
                 Have you never pondered on
                 the resemblance between
                 Beethoven and Sibelius?
                 And does not Rembrandt look like
                 Picasso, just a little bit?

Mina is not sure whether he is being serious or just
kidding her along.

MINA   And you, I suppose, are the
                 reincarnation of Casanova ...

DRACULA (roguishly) You understand, I am Casanova.

MINA (laughing) And I am Cleopatra and Juliet,
                 and Helen of Troy, and ...

DRACULA (interrupting, good-naturedly)
                 No you are not! You are
                 greater than all of those
                 and our love will be greater.
                 Tomorrow, at Castle Dracula,
                 it will be consummated.

MINA (half-seriously) At the cost of my soul.

DRACULA (lightly) What use to me is your soul.
                 God is welcome to it. Can your
                 soul savour the fragrance of a
                 rose, taste the liquid sunshine
                 of honey, feel the warm caress
                 of a summer breeze? Slough off
                 your soul like a snake its winter
                 skin and bask in the sun with me,
                 forever.

She is totally seduced and clasps Dracula in an eager embrace.

MINA   Forever! Forever!

As Dracula kisses, bites, then draws blood from her
neck, Mina imagines she is bedecked in a silver wed-
ding dress rising in her lover's arms to the stars.

DISSOLVE TO:

INT. COUNTRY CHAPEL. DAY.

Pan down from a simple crucifix to reveal a PRIEST
saying mass for a small CONGREGATION of PEASANTS.
Suddenly JONATHAN staggers in, unkempt, unshaven
and bedraggled as befits a man who has endured a
night's forced march across rough country. Without
ceremony he walks up the aisle and addresses the
startled priest.

JONATHAN   Father, I'm sorry - forgive me
                but I must ask you to bless this.

From his coat he takes the Winchester and holds it
out towards the Priest who thinks his life is being
threatened.

PRIEST (in Romanian) We are a poor community.
                Put your gun away my son; there
                is nothing worth taking here.

Aware that he is not getting through, Jonathan turns
to the congregation in desperation.

JONATHAN   Can someone help me please?
                I need your priest to bless this gun.

The silence is uncomprehending and total.

JONATHAN   Does no one understand?

Finally, when Jonathan is about to turn away, a dis-
tinguished looking man, probably a LANDOWNER, suddenly
speaks to the priest.

LANDOWNER (in Romanian) This man is deranged.
                He asks your blessing on his rifle.

The Priest regains some of his composure.

PRIEST (in Romanian) It would be the violation
                of a sacrament. Tell him No!
                It is blasphemy!

The landowner translates with discretion.

LANDOWNER   Why do you commit this blasphemy?

JONATHAN   I ask his blessing for good, not evil.

The play for words is over. The next instant Jonathan has taken aim, fired, and blown the top off one of the altar candles.

JONATHAN   There's no time for explanation.

Walking towards the Priest, he points the gun at him.

JONATHAN   Bless it! For Christ's sake, bless it!

An old man cries, and some women in the congregation start to whimper, the Priest crosses himself and trembling, blesses the outstretched rifle.

PRIEST   In nomine patris, et filii,
              et Spiritu Sanctu, Amen.

JONATHAN   God bless you.

Jonathan goes out of the back door leaving a great commotion behind him.

EXT. RIVERSIDE ROAD. DAY.

QUINCEY drives a mud-spattered sports car faster than safety permits down a narrow bumpy road while DR. SEWARD suffering at his side does his best to scan the lake through a pair of binoculars.

DR. SEWARD   Nearly there and not a sign.
              I'm sure they must have got
              him on the train.

QUINCEY   Fine! That still leaves the vampires
             at the Castle to take care of.

DR. SEWARD   Only if we find them before
              sunset. Stop! I've seen something
              ... it's too bumpy, stop! Take
              a look yourself.

Quincey stops the car and takes the binoculars.

QUINCEY's POINT OF VIEW: A large raft of logs in the centre of which, clearly visible, is Dracula's casket. Around it HALF A DOZEN GYPSY BANDITS keep watch and tend the horses while TWO MORE steer the craft round the rocks as it drifts downstream at about five knots. Quincey lowers the binoculars and turns urgently to DR. SEWARD.

QUINCEY   Goddamit, they failed!

DR. SEWARD   Then it's up to us, old man.
                 I'm not much of a shot I'm afraid.

QUINCEY   Time we picked a couple off,
                 the rest'd be hoppin' in back of
                 that basket like a bunch o' crickets.

DR. SEWARD   Too chancy, we've got to finish
                 him off for good. What's that?

The rumble of an explosion is heard.

QUINCEY   Sounds mighty like blastin'.

DR. SEWARD   Wasn't there a quarry back
                 there a mile or so?

QUINCEY   Yahoo! We'll blow the varmin' to
                 Kingdom come. Hold onto yer hat!

Dr. Seward smiles and nods in agreement as Quincey spins the car round and sets off back the way they came, so the raft continues on its journey.

EXT. RAFT. DAY.

One of the cloaked figures on board seems particularly interested in the casket. It is MINA attired as a bandit.

EXT. QUARRY. DAY:

QUINCEY helps the FOREMAN load explosives into the trunk, and then joins DR. SEWARD who is studying a map on the bonnet.

QUINCEY	First object accomplished. Now to clip his wings.
DR. SEWARD	By my reckoning, the raft is only five miles from the Castle.
QUINCEY	And the road follows the river all the way - they're going to see us, gosh darn'd it!
DR. SEWARD	Unless ... Look, the river forms an ox-bow here - doubles back on itself. If we could cut across country we'd stand a good chance of arriving ahead of them. That's if the terrain is suitable.
QUINCEY	There's only one way to find out, Doc.

Quincey slaps him excitedly on the back, jumps in the car and revs up. Map in hand Dr. Seward joins him looking rather worried.

DR. SEWARD	Those explosives, Quincey. They are safe, I presume?

Quincey laughs and throws the car into gear.

QUINCEY	You do the navigatin', Doc, and I'll do the prayin'.

Dr. Seward tightens his lips as the car backfires, and then drives out of the quarry. The rapport between them is growing. The car quickly turns off the road up a bumpy cart track which winds up a wild hillside. With a great splash it fords a mountain stream after which the primitive track soon ends. They careen wildly with many bumps and jolts through a forest of fir trees. When finally Dr. Seward calls a halt both men are feeling mentally and physically shaken as they thankfully get out of the car to unload.

EXT. CLIFF SUMMIT. DAY

From a vantage point is a wild jutting crag of rock overhanging a river several hundred feet below. On the opposite side of the ravine, Castle Dracula towers above them. As they peer over the edge and see the raft passing almost beneath them, they realise the urgency of the situation.

QUINCEY   What did you do in the war, Doc?

DR. SEWARD   Medical officer with the Surrey's.

QUINCEY   Didn't get to lob many grenades,
               I guess.

DR. SEWARD   No, but I bowled for Surrey Cricket
               Club for a couple of seasons.

QUINCEY (laughing) Silly mid on, short leg
               and all that stuff, huh?
               Boy! This takes me right
               back to Vlimey Ridge.

Without further delay they take a charge each and, having inserted and lit the fuse wire, lob their improvised bombs into space totally unaware that Mina's life is at risk. POW! POW! Two wasted shots exploding harmlessly in the air and alerting the BANDITS to danger.

DR. SEWARD   More fuse!

QUINCEY   An inch should do it.

They cut the fuses accordingly a little longer, and try again.

EXT. THE RAFT. DAY.

MINA and the BANDITS watch the charges fall into the river a few feet away then dive for cover as they explode and drench the casket with water. The Bandits prepare to open fire.

EXT. SUMMIT. DAY.

DR. SEWARD has trouble igniting his last charge so QUINCEY goes it alone only to be hit in the shoulder by a bullet before he has a chance to throw the bomb.

Spluttering, it drops at his feet as he staggers to retain his balance. The next instant, Dr. Seward hurls himself at Quincey knocking him off his feet and rolling with him behind a rock just as the charge explodes. Smoke obliterates everything for a moment but when it clears we see the two men are safe but dust-covered, though Quincey is bleeding from his wound.

QUINCEY   Guess it's up to you partner.
             Clean bowl him, centre stump.

DR. SEWARD   The wind's causing them
             to break wide. I'll put a
             spin on this one.

In saying this, he runs to the edge amid flying bullets and bowls a beauty. POW! A direct hit on the bow. Smoke and spray.

EXT. RAFT. DAY.

When the smoke clears the splintered logs are beginning to separate and drift apart. Those not killed by the explosion find themselves in the water and either holding onto a log for support or struggling to safety. Most lucky of all is MINA, still unrecognizable in her bandit garb, she has grabbed the mane of a horse swimming towards the bank. As for the casket, it sinks undamaged beneath the water.

EXT. SUMMIT. DAY.

QUINCEY crawls towards DR. SEWARD who is lying on his chest near the edge of the precipice peering through binoculars.

DR. SEWARD   Offside stump, I'm afraid.

Quincey takes the binoculars and scans the swirling water. There is no sign of Dracula.

QUINCEY   Well, he's 'out' all the same.

DR. SEWARD (reluctantly) Dracula, the man, will
             most certainly drown, but after

127

sunset he becomes supernatural -
able to change into God knows what.

QUINCEY (ruefully) Heck, don't tell me I
should'a brought my fishin' line!

EXT. THE RIVER BED. DAY.

Bubbles inside the casket imprisoned in a bed of
drifting weed. Fingers slowly emerge from beneath
the lid struggling ineffectually to raise it. The
bubbles die in volume as the struggling hand grows
weaker, till suddenly the fingers have vanished and
in their place a WATER RAT wriggles out and starts
swimming to the surface.

DISSOLVE TO:

EXT. THE RIVER BANK. DAY.

The WATER RAT swims to shore, scrambles over some
rocks and disappears into the undergrowth only to
emerge a moment later transformed into a Vampire
BAT flying towards the Castle high above the hilltop.

EXT. CASTLE DRACULA. DAY.

MINA stands on the battlements, hair blowing in the
wind, transfigured by love and desire as she watches the BAT winging its way closer and closer to her
outstretched arms. CRACK! A shot rings out. She
looks around in panic and sees the barrel of a Winchester protruding from the top of a nearby turret.
As another shot is fired at the approaching Vampire,
she turns and runs up a flight of stone steps towards
the Marksman.

JONATHAN gets in another shot just as Mina appears
and hurls herself at him sharp teeth bared in hatred. The rifle goes spinning from his hands as the
unharmed BAT flies closer and closer.

JONATHAN   Mina, for God's sake,
                it's our only chance,
                he must be destroyed!

EXT. SUMMIT. DAY.

DR. SEWARD   How's the shoulder?

QUINCEY   Busted I guess ...

Dr. Seward rips off Quincey's shirt sleeve and examines
the wound.

DR. SEWARD   You're lucky. The bullet passed
              clean through.

He tears the sleeve into strips and starts bandaging
the shoulder.

QUINCEY   My turn to do a little bleedin'
              anyways.

DR. SEWARD (laughing) Let's hope it will be
              the last ...
              (but suddenly his face clouds)
              I say Quincey, I've just had a
              terrible thought. What time is it?

Quincey looks at his wrist-watch, frowns and shakes it.

QUINCEY   Heck, it stopped at 5:45.

DR. SEWARD   Sunset in this longitude
              is 5:51. Of course that's
              at sea level; up here it
              would be a few minutes later.

He looks at the heavy low cloud for any sign of a
break. Quincey loses something of his jubilation.

QUINCEY   What are you tryin' to tell me,
              Doc? He's a goner, ain't he?

EXT. CASTLE DRACULA. DAY.

MINA   No, you shall not harm him!
              You shall not!

Mina tears at Jonathan like a wild cat frustrating
all his efforts to retrieve the gun. Meanwhile, the

BAT is within a few feet of them, homing in towards
Jonathan for the kill when suddenly the clouds part
revealing the sun sinking behind distant mountains
throwing out one last golden ray to strike down the
grim black bat.
His supernatural power gone, DRACULA becomes a helpless
naked man flapping his arms in the sky, falling like
Icarus, a victim of the sun's majesty. With a scream
like a shriek from hell, Dracula plummets down towards
the dead pine trees at the foot of the castle wall,
impaled at last like hundreds of his hapless victims
before him.

Mina, who has watched the fall of her vampire lover,
transfixed, screams and collapses into Jonathan's
arms. Snatching up his gun on the way, Jonathan
carries the unconscious Mina down the turret steps.

INT. CASTLE DRACULA. THE GREAT HALL. DUSK.

JONATHAN carries MINA down the spiral staircase and
is making for the front door when a sound causes him
to spin round. One of the VAMPIRE WOMEN is running
towards him.

FIRST VAMPIRE WOMAN Stop! Stop!

Slipping Mina into a chair, Jonathan takes aim and
shoots the Vampire through the heart with a sacred
bullet. She falls, true dead, on the floor, the oil
lamp she was holding tumbles onto some heavy drapery
which instantly ignites. A moment later her TWO SISTERS
appear at the far end of the corridor and run forward
to the wall of flame. Jonathan is about to take aim
for a second time when the SECOND VAMPIRE speaks to
him through the flames. By now, Mina is coming round
and is also witness to her words.

SECOND VAMPIRE WOMAN There is nothing to fear,
                    put down your gun. We are free now.
                    Our sister was trying to thank you.
                    Dracula has no dominion over us.
                    His evil power died with him.
                    What prize the quest for eternal
                    beauty when the cost is counted
                    in innocent lives.

THIRD VAMPIRE WOMAN Fear of death holds
                   less dread for us than fear
                   of life. To live eternally
                   without love is to know the
                   true meaning of damnation.

SECOND VAMPIRE WOMAN To live eternally without
                    love is to suffer all the agonies
                    of hell!

SECOND/THIRD VAMPIRE WOMAN (in unison)
                   He could not love. He could not love!

Mina, who has been deeply moved, leaps up with
compassion.

MINA   May God forgive you,
             may He forgive us all.

She is crying as Jonathan leads her to the door,
watching the redeemed vampires finding peace in the
flames.

EXT. CASTLE DRACULA. THE COURTYARD. DAY.

The sports car containing DR. SEWARD and QUINCEY
circles the courtyard as JONATHAN and MINA stagger
out of the door followed by billowing clouds of
smoke. Climbing into the car with all possible
haste, they are soon speeding over the drawbridge
and down the hill.

EXT. ROADWAY. DUSK.

As the car carrying the FOUR ADVENTURERS flashes
past, the CAMERA whips to the dead fir tree on which
DRACULA is impaled. His face withered and distorted
by 500 years of mania is set in a look of crazed disbelief as his Castle blazes above him like a giant
torch in the darkening sky.

- THE END -

Postscript

Among the correspondence I've received since the publication of Ken Russell's script was a letter from an established novelist and illustrator who was surprised that Ken Russell allowed the 'hearties' to defeat 'The Artist'. "Maltreated though he was as an artist, Ken must have known that however much the philistines may trample on Beauty as something alien to them and therefore threatening, the creative spirit will ultimately survive triumphant in spite of them." He enclosed the following suggestion as an alternative ending, constructed around a character Russell created for the adaptation, and has given me permission to publish it.

Readers are welcome to send in 'additional scenes' and illustrations. The most interesting examples will be published in future editions.

KEN RUSSELL's DRACULA, ALTERNATIVE ENDING

EXT. ROAD WAY. DUSK.

As the car carrying the FOUR ADVENTURERS flashes past, the CAMERA whips to the dead fir tree on which DRACULA is impaled. His face withered and distorted by 500 years of mania is set in a look of crazed disbelief as his Castle blazes above him like a giant torch in the darkening sky.]

EXT. FIR FOREST CLEARING. BRIGHT NIGHT.

Naked and silvered with moonlight, the GARDENER'S BOY seems almost afloat as he stands looking upward.

BOY (half adoringly, half Puckishly)
        I come, Master, I come to you,
        and shall release you. DISSOLVE TO:

DRACULA'S FACE, which relaxes as he hears the Boy's voice. He listens intently. The red firelight is diminishing.

DISSOLVE TO:

EXT. FIR FOREST CLEARING. BRIGHT NIGHT.

BOY (still adoringly, but even more roguishly)
        I shall release you with a kiss.
        (he grins)
        Oh, how we fool them, these
        mortal men with their stakes
        and crosses, and these mortal
        women who believe themselves
        beloved by their Casanova.
        How we feast on their folly,
        you and I.

A tinkling cascade of laughter breaks from him and his teeth show like sudden sharp pearls in the moonlight. A thin trickle of blood runs down the length of his pale torso from his mouth to his groin as if he has bitten his own lip.

DISSOLVE TO:

DRACULA'S FACE, which is now cleared of all pain, and alert with anticipation. The red firelight has all but faded away.

DISSOLVE TO:

The BOY, still upright, is now almost perceptibly floating upward against a background of stars and fir branches.

BOY   (adoringly as before, but never solemn,
                more as if grinning with pride)
               I come, Master, for my spirit is yours.
               I am Ariel.
               I am Hermes.
               I am the spirit of inspiration
               and you are the Creator.
               My body and blood are yours.
               For I am Ganymede.
               The Boy of the Sonnets.
               I am Eros Triumphant.
               I shall release you with
               a kiss and creep close
               beneath your cloak.
               For you and I are One,
               Master. Forever.

DISSOLVE TO:

DRACULA'S FACE. His eyes now seem to see the Boy clearly and to watch his off-camera approach. The back of the BOY'S BLOND HEAD floats into the frame until it covers the face of DRACULA. A long moment. When the BOY'S HEAD withdraws again, DRACULA'S FACE is rejuvenated and transfigured. There is blood on his lips.

DRACULA (whispers) Forever.

DRACULA too now seems to float free and upward as the CAMERA cuts slightly back. Fir branches give way entirely to stars. The light is no longer red, all is now luminous silver and black. Though both figures remain upright, the floating effect increases as the BOY slips beneath DRACULA's cloak and against his chest. As his cloak closes behind the BOY like a theatre curtain, DRACULA smiles.

- THE END -

Also Published by Buffalo Books:

TALKING ABOUT KEN RUSSELL by Paul Sutton
This landmark book, more than a decade in the making, contains hundreds of exclusive interviews with Russell and the people who worked with him, and includes, for example, the first-hand testimonies of more than a dozen people who worked on *Women in Love*, and twenty-three members of the cast and crew of *The Devils*. Actors, editors, designers, continuity women, producers, assistants, special effects artists, composers, sound recordists, and the camera crews, all recall their working days with Ken Russell. In addition to these interviews, Paul Sutton adds choice finds from his research into Russell's careers in photography, film and opera, and uncovers a treasure trove of previously unknown material. This book aims to shine new light on the popular masterpieces and bring to the fore lesser-known works that should be better-known. 978-0993177040 566 pages Large format hardback. Lavishly illustrated in colour (b&w version also available)

BECOMING KEN RUSSELL by Paul Sutton
Using years of interviews with Russell and his colleagues, and unearthing thousands of previously unpublished documents, this tells the full story of Ken Russell's rise through ballet, photography, and amateur films to become a professional independent filmmaker. Sutton details the day-by-day, almost frame-by-frame, making of Russell's first 35mm films commissioned by the BBC, and which redefined the meaning of 'English Cinema'. 978-0-9572462-6-3 paperback. Illustrated (b&w)

TO EACH HIS OWN DOLCE VITA by John Francis Lane
Deciding not to come of age in a war-broken England facing decades of austerity, John Francis Lane chose to settle in Rome where he followed the blossoming of the 'dolce vita' before it was given a name in Federico Fellini's masterpiece, in which Lane appeared, and for which he would be entrusted by Fellini to supervise the English-language version. He cameoed in films by Antonioni, Pier Paolo Pasolini and many others; and he met everyone who was anyone passing through or living in the Italy of those years, from Visconti to Orson Welles, Franco Zeffirelli, De Sica, John Wayne, Sophia Loren, Sean Connery, Marlene Dietrich, Gore Vidal, Antia Ekberg, De Filippo, Dario Fo, Anna Magnani, Francesco Rosi, Lindsay Anderson, Bette Davis, Laurence Olivier, Dino De Laurentiis, Richard Fleischer, Steve Reeves, Rock Hudson, Alberto Moravia, Vittorio Gassman, David O'Selznick, Monica Vita, Warren Beatty, David O'Selznick, Gina Lollobrigida.
The deliciously honest, occasionally profound and often amusing memoirs of an Englishman abroad, who was knighted for his services to Italian arts. 400 pages - Illustrated

FALLING UPWARDS by Tim Dry
Tim Dry's virtuoso memoir of a life in arts. It rises and falls through the worlds of art school and mime and New Romantics pop to the cinema of *Star Wars* and the theatre of Steven Berkoff; hallucinogenic drugs; internationally-prized photography and a globetrottery of commercials. From a childhood encounter with a UFO to playing an alien in the cult film, *Xtro*; from seeing The Beatles as a boy to befriending Angie Bowie and performing in front of 100,000 people with Gary Numan. Tim Dry breaks into a theatre to see Kate Bush; makes a highwire appearance on stage with Duran Duran; photographs Mick Jagger; is paid to go berserk as a robot in Germany; has a week-long near nude scene in a film with Ann-Margret; and presents a food programme on Channel 4. All this and much, much more.
978-0-9572462-6-3   Paperback illustrated

GARY NUMAN, AN ANNOTATED SCRAPBOOK by Paul Sutton
Gary Numan was one of the first pop artists to place equal emphasis on image and sound, a true Warholian artist who advanced on Andy's light and sound experiments with The Velvet Underground, by bringing a real grandeur to live performances, and by changing the music of the world with a single finger. This book collects together articles from England, America, Japan, Spain, Italy and Germany, to give a clear picture of the first years of fame of the modest young Englishman, and which show, for example, that Numan's 1979 album *Replicas* is the missing link between the novel *Do Androids Dream of Electric Sheep?* and the film *Blade Runner*.
Large format hardback 978-0993177071 320 pages. Lavishly illustrated

UNDERSTANDING GARY NUMAN by Paul Sutton
In this small paperback produced to accompany the *Annotated Scrapbook,* the historian, Paul Sutton explains the importance of Gary Numan on music. He takes the reader through a vastly entertaining potted history of rock music pioneers, tracing them all back to "a bayou swamp or a delta of Mississippi mud from where howled the first wolf and harmonica, and from where was heard the first blue plucking finger on string", to show that "popular music was strictly The Imitation Game" until Gary Numan came along with his Machine Quartet, four albums that re-invigorated rock and roll. "Numan's music added so many new strands of DNA to the gene pool of what hitherto had been dead Mississippi mud that the transformative effect was immediate and everlasting."
114 pages (hardback). 978-0993177088 Paperback version also available

33571535R00083